CAPTIVE FLAMES

MONSIGNOR RONALD KNOX

CAPTIVE FLAMES

*On Selected Saints
and Christian Heroes*

IGNATIUS PRESS   SAN FRANCISCO

Original edition published 1940 by Burns Oates
Published with ecclesiastical permission
New edition printed by permission of the Earl of
Oxford and Asquith, care of A. P. Watt Limited

Cover art:

Pope St. Gregory Dictating His
Writings to His Scribe Peter (detail)
from *Moralium in Job* of St. Gregory
France, 12th c., Ms. 79, f. 57
Bibliotheque Municipale, Laon, France
© Giraudon/Art Resource, New York

Cover design by Roxanne Mei Lum

Published in 2001 by
Ignatius Press, San Francisco
ISBN 0–89870–836–2
Library of Congress Control Number: 2001088855
Printed in the United States of America ∞

Dedication
to
Arnold Lunn

DEAR ARNOLD,

You are always complaining that I do not give you copies of my books; so I have determined to manœuvre for a superior position by dedicating this to you. You will complain at once that a collection of old sermons is a poor sort of book, hardly a book at all. To be sure, nothing is more dated than your old sermons—especially occasional sermons, like these. Their associations were local, the impulse of ecclesiastical festivity which inspired them is not easily recaptured; your own style, your own taste, have changed, and these past utterances hardly seem to belong to you. Besides, what is not dated, that was written between 1919 and 1939? Those two decades of our lives will perhaps be remembered in history only as an uneasy twilight; we cannot tell, whether of dusk or dawn.

And yet, though all the setting of these sermons be fugitive, the main theme of them is something which does not alter with our shifting perspectives, does not grow old. The saints do not belong to a period; there is a cousinship between St. Cecily talking to the angel Valerian could not see, and St. Bernadette kneeling at the foot of the rock, apparently all alone. They are fixed stars, not subject to any law of impermanence. And this book is about saints; a puddle reflecting their star-shine. Only,

I found that I had included one about Henry the Sixth, who was never canonized, in the hope that he would not arouse any Harrovian prejudice in you; and one about Roger Bacon, no saint but an Oxford scientist—I know you are patient with scientists, and Oxford has a meaning for you. So I thought I would round off the number of these sermons, for luck, with the sermon I think I am most proud to have preached; the panegyric uttered in Westminster Cathedral, when you and I and all our contemporaries lost, in Chesterton, the oracle of our youth.

One of the sermons was preached to undergraduates (you have preached to undergraduates); several to schoolboys; not all of them, therefore, have the dignity which some people associate with the pulpit. But I put them in, leaving them just as they were, in the hope that one or two people might pick up the book here and there, who had been present when one of those sermons was delivered, and so cheat themselves for a moment with the illusion of living in the past. That, for all men is a transitory relief; though their memory does not go back to such fine days as ours.

Such as it is, then, here it is; and never say that I did not dedicate a book to you.

R. A. K.

ALDENHAM, 1940

Contents

8   CAPTIVE FLAMES

I

St. Cecilia

(*Preached at St. Anselm and St. Cecilia's, Kingsway*)

In like manner also, let wives be subject to their husbands: that, if any believe not the word, they may be won without the word, by the conversation of the wives, considering your chaste conversation with fear (1 Pet 3:1).

THE LEGENDS of the early Roman Saints, among whom your holy patroness St. Cecilia is numbered, do not always command great attention from the critically minded historian. The records, he will tell you, were compiled at an uncertain date, but a date very much later than the events they deal with; the miracles in them are purposelessly elaborate; the tone of them rather suggests that they have been written up for the edification of pious readers. That is all very well, but every now and again you meet with curious evidences of the accuracy of these Roman traditions, and not least in the case of St. Cecilia herself. A little time ago they dug underneath the Church of St. Cecilia across the Tiber, to find out whether there was any justification for the tradition that that church was built on the site of St. Cecilia's house. And sure enough it proved that St. Cecilia's, like St. Clement's, was built over an old Roman house. But there was more than that —there is one chapel in the church which was always supposed to be the exact site of St. Cecilia's martyrdom.

9

In the story, you will remember, St. Cecilia was finally put to death in a bath. And just underneath the chapel of the martyrdom, so I am told, in the structure of the old Roman house, they found the traces of the old Roman apparatus for heating the bath water. Which shows that we ought to be very careful about how we disbelieve the Roman legends.

But whether the story of St. Cecilia as it is told in her acts is all true or only partly true, there is a simplicity about the whole story and a simplicity about St. Cecilia's character in the story which demands that anyone who stands in the pulpit on an occasion like this should preach a simple sermon about her. She is not like that other great Virgin Martyr, St. Catherine of Alexandria. St. Catherine of Alexandria was a great philosopher, according to the story, who confounded all the thinkers of Alexandria by the acuteness of her apologetics. And, though I have every respect for St. Catherine as the patroness of my own College, I do imagine St. Catherine as a rather formidable person to meet; she would, I fancy, lecture on Catholic Evidence platforms. But there is nothing of that about St. Cecilia, although she is full of zeal for her religion; her public is the home, her platform the breakfast table. I hope it is not necessary to remind you, except in the most general way, of her story—how she was married to a young pagan called Valerian, but persuaded him to respect her vow of virginity, because her guardian Angel would make him sorry for it if he did otherwise: how Valerian wanted to see this guardian Angel, but Cecilia, with her innocent craft, said he could not do that unless he was baptized first; how he was baptized, and saw the

Angel at her side as she prayed; how he made a convert of his brother Tiburtius, and how first the two brothers, and then Cecilia herself, were punished with death for professing the Christian religion. It is an old story, and a familiar one: and while we do all homage to St. Catherine for her courage in lecturing in the parks, we shall always need St. Cecilia as well, quietly working at home for the conversion of her own husband and his family.

Not that St. Cecilia herself was in the position of a modern wife. Like so many Christian ladies of her time, she had taken, in imitation of our Blessed Lady, a vow of perpetual virginity. When you read of the Virgin Martyrs you must not think of that connection of titles as an accidental one; that certain martyrs happened to be virgins or certain virgins happened to be martyrs. They were martyrs because they were virgins: it was because they insisted on keeping their vow when their parents wished them to marry that the secret of their attachment to the Christian faith was discovered; and it was their persistency in maintaining it that led to their martyrdom. It would be hard to estimate, I think, how much of its unpopularity in Roman society the Christian faith owed to its tradition of virginity. You know the horror the world feels when somebody becomes a Catholic; you know the horror the world feels when somebody goes into a convent: combine those two, and transplant them into a society which is heathen and regards the Christian religion as a dangerous and debased cult and you will realize what the pagans thought of a resolution like St. Cecilia's.

Virginity is an ideal which the pagans had no right to misunderstand. For, in theory, they, too, honoured it; and it should have commended itself to their heathen instinct for sacrifice. For the point of a sacrifice is that the victim should be spotless, the best of its kind. You must offer not what you can well afford to spare, but what will cost you something. The victim must be young, not old, perfect, not mutilated; pure bred, not of inferior stock: it is the fairest flower that must wither in front of the statue. That is the pagan idea of sacrifice; and the Christian idea of sacrifice is based on the same principle. In order to give up something to God, we forgo, not the sinful pleasures which we have no right to in any case, but the lawful pleasures which he has given us to enjoy if we will. And it is not broken hearts or wasted careers that produce vocations to the religious life. It is the young, the attractive, the brilliant, those who have the fullest life and the highest hopes before them, who make the perfect sacrifice when they devote themselves to Almighty God in holy religion.

The pagans ought to have understood that; our modern world does not; it simply talks about waste. Well, I am not going to argue that now: I am only pointing out that Catholics, in whatever age of the world, must think of the life of virginity as the highest vocation of all. But for this morning, let us think of St. Cecilia rather as an example to people living in the world, a patroness of the home. Hers was a mixed marriage; of course, she could not help herself; parents in her day had all the arrangement of such matters in their hands, and presumably her parents were not Christians. Do not let us run away with the impression that all Catholics ought to make mixed marriages, in order to bring fresh families into the Church. There is at least as much harm done to the Church by mixed marriages as good; at least as much harm. And there is no doubt that, in the eyes of the Church, such marriages are an unfortunate necessity that you cannot avoid, not an ideal to be aimed at. A Catholic who means to marry, but has not (so to speak) filled in the name yet, ought to mean, God willing, to marry a Catholic. But mixed marriages, I suppose, will always go on; and at any rate we have to allow for the case where, after marriage, the husband or the wife becomes a convert, but not both. The same situation arises—a difference of creed within the four walls of the same house. And it is there that St. Cecilia ought to help us.

What won her husband to the faith, in spite of his passion, in spite (you might almost say) of his love for her, was the purity of her nature which, though a heathen, he could already discern. His eyes were not yet open to the supernatural world that rules and interpenetrates ours; he could not see the Angel until he was baptized. But he could see, in his Christian bride, a new experience in his life—a blinding flash of purity. And the first duty of a Catholic wife or a Catholic husband, if they would redeem the promise they made to labour for husband's or for wife's conversion, is to be a model of Christian purity. The religious life, the life of virginity, is not for them; they have made their choice. But within the holy bond of matrimony, the Catholic has to hold up the highest possible standard of faithfulness—faithfulness both to the person of the other partner in the marriage, and to the will of God in designing matrimony for the procreation of children. Let husband or wife be won to the faith by the behaviour of wife or husband, by considering the chasteness of that behaviour with fear. The world knows that Catholics have a high standard of purity. But the world is not going to be impressed unless it is assured that Catholics keep it.

And that is not only a lesson for wives and husbands; it is a lesson for all of us. The purity which is our traditional inheritance as Catholics has a message and a charm for the world about us. Each of us, whether he likes it or not, is an advertisement of the Catholic faith to the little circle of his neighbours—a good advertisement, or a bad advertisement. And it is such a mistake to think that we ought to try and impress our neighbours by making it clear to them that Catholics are not Puritans, are not strait-laced, are sportsmen like anybody else. The world is very ready to say that of us, but it does not really respect us for it. It does not respect us, for being ready to join in rather risky conversation, and enjoy rather doubtful jokes; it does not respect us for being careless about what company we keep and what places of amusement we go to. It respects us, if it sees that we shrink from the touch of anything that may defile us; if it sees that the virginity which is practised in the cloister has its complement and its fruit in the chaste conversation of Catholics who are living in the world.

So, while St. Anselm's feast reminds us to be loyal sons of the Church, ready to hold the faith and to defend the faith in life and in death, let St. Cecilia's feast remind us to take our Christian vocation seriously, to follow out in our lives the words we profess with our lips. And may both, English bishop and Roman maiden, pray for you who worship here and for those who minister to you, that when Christ, the Master they served, comes again in judgement, you may be found blameless before Almighty God.

II

St. George

All mirth is forsaken; the joy of the earth is gone away (Is 24:11).

WE ARE celebrating to-night the Feast of St. George, the heavenly patron of England. I do not mean to derive any lesson from the life or from the martyrdom of St. George, because it appears that nothing whatever is known about either. We were all brought up on the story of St. George and the Dragon, but these historians who spoil all our nursery romances tell us that this is quite untrue: indeed, the Church has very prudently refrained from giving any sanction to the legend of the Saint, and has officially declared him to be one of those holy men whose actions are known only to God. Instead, we will occupy ourselves this evening in thinking about England. I say England, not the United Kingdom, or the British Empire. St. George is not the patron of the United Kingdom, or of the British Empire. He is the patron of these strange folk that live between the Severn and the Wash, between the Tweed and the English Channel; a folk honest, on the whole, kindly, on the whole, shy, a little surly, law-abiding, but doggedly tenacious of their rights, rather too self-satisfied, incurably sentimental, dreadfully muddle-headed. He is the patron of that country of chalk downs, of little fields bordered by green

17

hedges, of wandering lanes, of hills scarcely rising above
the level of cultivation, of old trees and of long manorial
tenure, which we call England. I do not flatter myself
by supposing that this congregation consists of entirely
English stock; I conceive it to be probable that there are
one or two of you, scattered about here and there, whose
blood thrills to a different music, whose loyalties have
their focus on the other side of that channel which we
have so strangely dedicated to St. George. I cannot help
that; you are a month late for St. Patrick's Day. You will
have to be honorary Englishmen for this evening.

It is a peculiarity of the English that they do most things
in a vague, haphazard, untidy sort of way, without being
able to give any particular reasons for doing it. And nothing is more characteristic of them than their choice of a
patron saint. There was no conceivable reason why it
should have been St. George more than anybody else.
There is no ground for thinking that St. George had ever
been in England; it is not even certain, I suppose, that he
had ever heard of England. He was represented in popular
legend as being a soldier, but England is not, and never
was, a military nation by choice. We just picked him up,
somehow, in the Crusades, and that was all there was to it.
I doubt, even, whether there was a great popular devotion
to the Saint in the Middle Ages. A fairly large number
of parish churches are dedicated to him, but not many, I
think, date beyond the Reformation. And I could show
you a list of one hundred and fifty country people in the
later Middle Ages out of whom only three bear George
as their baptismal name. Its real popularity, I fancy, dates
from those one hundred and seventeen continuous years

of English history during which George was the King's name.

But there is one phrase we all of us know which does, in a curious way, identify our national Saint with the memory of our remote forefathers, I mean the war cry, the slogan we should call it: 'Saint George for merry England!' For *merry* England—when I say that there is no trace of a popular medieval devotion to the Saint, I must admit on the other side the great popularity of The George and Dragon as a sign over inn doors. In that most essentially English of our institutions, the country inn, our national Saint does seem to have come to his own. He has passed, somehow, into that tradition of hearty good-fellowship, of beef-eating and beer-drinking jollity, of which Chaucer first hymned the praises, and Charles Dickens wrote the epitaph. Merry England—it is hard to see why they should have been so merry. The country was devastated by wars, civil wars mostly; the great plague of the Black Death made whole tracts of the country-side into a wilderness; there were cruel landlords, there were worldly priests, there was poverty, and loose living, and crime. But, somehow, to these forefathers of ours, the England for which they fought was a merry England; it smiled to them across the seas, as they fell at Crécy and Agincourt, in a haze of fun and good comradeship.

Merry England—do we talk much about 'merry England' now? If you open your morning paper, and cast your eye down the news—strikes, divorce actions, murders, unemployment statistics, grave warnings to the public, and similar matter that chiefly occupy its pages—is merry the first word that rises to your lips? Oh, I know, we are gay, we are frivolous, we hurl ourselves into our pleasures. No expense can be too heavy for producing a film, for putting on a revue, for hiring a football professional. We dance all night, and play tennis all day—those of us who have the leisure. But is there not something suspicious about this feverish gaiety of ours, about these demands for a brighter London, this dreary cry for the unsexing of women, these lurid posters that herald our public amusements? Does not our laughter ring rather hollow, as if we were making merry not because we feel light-hearted, but because we want to forget the anxieties that are weighing us down? Our industries, our trade, our empire, our birth-rate, our morals—do they encourage merriment? Our poetry, our clever novels, our art—do they reflect a mood of happiness? Our expert critics, do they bid us believe that all is well with England? Is our gaiety real, or is it a smile painted on the face of a corpse?

Oh, I am not going to talk politics. I am not going to discuss how much of our present difficulties we owe to our ancestors, how much to ourselves, how much to circumstances that we could not have avoided. Even at this moment it is doubtful whether our merry England will have a merry month of May. It is no place of mine, here, to discuss such issues, unless perhaps to implore your prayers for the divine guidance of our rulers. I will not even remind you—the theme has become almost a trite one—how the landlordism that was born with the Reformation prepared the way for that terrible division of class interests which has been with us since the industrial revolution. I do not believe that in the last resort the moods of a country, its moods of depression, or of elation, of hope, or of despair, arise from economic causes or can be altered by material changes. Outward conditions do affect us, of course—a little at all times, violently at some times. But in the long run England will not be merry or sad because there is more coal or less coal, because there is more trade or less trade. Ultimately the spirit of man is the arbiter of his happiness; men will be merry or sad according as they have found their right place or their wrong place in the scheme of things; and peace between nations, peace between classes, will come only when man is at peace with himself, and at peace with God.

And England will not be merry until England is Catholic. That word 'merry' is not so simple as it sounds. It is a difficult word, for example, to translate into any foreign language. It is typical of our modern conditions that we hardly ever use it nowadays, except when we call a person 'merry,' meaning that he was slightly drunk. It survives, chiefly, in old-fashioned formulas such as Merry England, or a Merry Christmas. Merry does not mean drunk, or uproarious, or frivolous. It means that a man is light-hearted, that his mind is at ease, that he is in a good humour, that he is ready to share a bit of fun with his neighbours. There is humility in the word, and innocence, and comradeship. And such a frame of mind as that is not to be secured, by grown-up people, through a continuous whirl of excitements, or a long course of dissipations. It comes from within.

A country cannot be merry while it forgets God. And a country cannot be merry for long, or with safety, if it tries to be Christian without being Catholic. England is not,

of course, even to-day, a country of atheists. But there is
a very large fraction of our fellow-countrymen—I do not
think you can put it much lower than four-fifths—which
does not go to Church. And most of these people do not
think about God if they can help it—that is what I call
'forgetting God.' They try to satisfy themselves with this
world; and that is a thing which you cannot do; Almighty
God does not mean us to do it; he wants to draw us back
to himself. The man who confines his outlook to this
world is worried all the time, at the back of his mind, by
the old riddle of existence; the troubles, the sufferings,
the tragedies of the world keep flicking him like briers as
he goes along: problems of conduct—which is the right
thing to do, and why should I do it?—stick to him like
burrs and force themselves upon his notice. You may forget your cares for a time, you may drown them occasionally with your pleasures, but you can never banish them.
A man will never be light-hearted in this world unless he
is thinking of the next world; this world is too chequered
an affair for that.

And in the long run, even a Christian nation cannot
be merry unless it is a Catholic nation. For these non-
Catholic Christianities—why, I do not know, but as a
matter of observation it is true—always go hand-in-hand
with some kind of Puritanism that interferes with man's
innocent enjoyments. Sometimes they want to make us
all into teetotallers, sometimes they are out against box-
ing, or racing, or the stage; sometimes they insist that we
shall sit indoors all Sunday afternoon and go to sleep.
Wherever Protestant opinion really rules a country, you
always find legislation of one sort or another which is de-

signed to stop people being merry. It sounds distant and old-fashioned to us, but that is because Protestantism has lost its grip of the country. In the United States, where the Protestants, though few in number, are rich and powerful, the thing goes on to this day. And when Protestantism does lose its grip, a reaction sets in, a reaction against Puritanism, which instead of making people merry makes them dissolute. A false religion, no less than lack of religion, will destroy, in the end, a nation's peace of mind.

Let us comfort ourselves, then, those of us who love England, with the thought that in trying to convert England we are not trying to alter her into something that is strange and foreign: we are trying to make her once more merry England—that which she was and that which traditionally she ought to be. Those who hate our religion are fond of pointing us to the example of Catholic nations abroad, of which they draw a very unfair picture, and then say: 'Look at Belgium—do you want England to be like that? Look at Spain—do you want England to be like that?' But the truth is that, for better or worse, England will never be quite like any other country. You may love her, you may hate her, but you must take her as she stands. Those native virtues that now grow wild in her hedgerows will only bloom the stronger and the fairer when the faith cultivates them. The more England becomes Catholic, the more English she will become.

Let us, then, on this feast of our patron, pray earnestly and resolve always to pray earnestly for the conversion of the country we love. Let us ask his prayers, and the prayers of our Blessed Lady and the English martyrs, that the tide of conversions we see chronicled year by year may flow still more strong, and still more deep, till at last the heart of the country reawakes, and remembers, and returns to her ancient love. It will hardly be in our time, I suppose, that the change comes; but even now we can stand, like Moses on Mount Nebo, and see beneath us the promised land that is one day to be our Catholic heritage. Let us stand together, strong in the faith of that vision, and resolve that through no fault of ours, no lapse of ours, no neglect of ours, that high endeavour to which we are pledged shall fall short of a swift and a lasting achievement. May the prayers of St. George protect this country that is dedicated to his honour, and bring all those who do him honour to that true country of ours which is in heaven.

III

St. Gregory the Great

(*Preached to schoolboys at St. Edmund's, Ware*)

Now therefore you are no more strangers and foreigners,
but you are fellow citizens with the Saints (Eph 2:19).

I DO NOT know if we always pay quite enough attention,
except, of course, for the really big days, to the Saints
whose feasts come round year by year. The smaller ones
are apt to pass altogether unnoticed, and even the bigger
ones come suddenly and take us by surprise. The Saint I
want to speak of now is to-day's Saint, whose name, in
case you did not catch it when the Collect was sung, is
St. Gregory—St. Gregory the Great.

His name is derived from *egregora*, which, as the prefects
would tell you, is the strong perfect (with Attic redupli-
cation) of the Greek verb *egeiro*, to wake up. So St. Gregory is the wide-awake man, the man who is always on
the spot; there are no flies on him, as the Americans say.
I suppose the Church has seldom had a ruler who got
through more business. He wrote enormous quantities
of theology, and is counted as one of the four great Latin
doctors—you will see him pushing our Lord's chariot in
the picture in the *ambulacrum*. He was one of the great
early legislators of the Church, especially in matters of
liturgy. And all the time, a profound statesman, he was

25

guiding the destinies of the Church through a most difficult period of history, thinking nothing too insignificant
or too remote for his personal attention. And one of the
very remote and insignificant things he organized was the
conversion of an island somewhere off the coast of France,
called Britain. The Britons, in the classical authors, are
always used as a synonym for the extreme limit, the outside edge of mankind—those Britons, tucked away right
at the end of the world, much as we should say 'Borneo'
or 'Patagonia.' And I should think in St. Gregory's time,
owing to the invasion of the Angles and Saxons, England
was a still more inaccessible and unheard-of region. And
that is where St. Gregory sent St. Augustine to convert
you and me when we were little heathens.

Let us tell ourselves the story again, as the Venerable
Bede tells it us, and all the history books tell it in imitation of him. Just imagine that you are an English boy,
who went to the seaside and stayed on paddling when his
mother told him not to, and a lot of disreputable Danes,
coming back from a marauding expedition, bundled you,
a whole lot of you, on board their ship and sold you at
the nearest French port for the price of a drink. And then
you have drifted about from one slave-dealer to another all
over Europe, and finally you are standing about in a large
market-place at Rome, in the very centre of the world.
You are looking bored and sulky, and there is a placard
over your head to say: 'This size £12.' And then a stranger
comes up, and says something to the slave-dealer, obviously something like: 'Poor kids!' A very kind-looking
gentleman this, all dressed in a long black gown. And he
asks who you are, and the man says: 'Angles,' and you

expect the same old joke you've heard all over Europe, about your looking rather obtuse Angles, but no! it doesn't come. It's quite a new one this time. 'Angles! You mean Angels? That's the right name for them; at least, they look like Angels, and it's a pity they are not fellow-citizens of the Angels in heaven. What part of Anglia do they come from?' 'Oh, from Deiri.' 'Well, they ought to be saved *de ira Dei*'—you probably will not understand that joke, since it is in Latin, but the bystanders seem to find it very funny. 'And what is their king called?' The kind gentleman does not have quite such luck this time; their king is called Aella. However, he does his best, and says something about what a good thing it would be if Aella's subjects learned to sing Alleluia. And they all laugh again; only the kind gentleman goes on his way looking rather serious.

Well, of course, the kind gentleman was St. Gregory. He was a very holy man, but he did not mind making jokes; there is hope in that for all of us. And he was a very clever man, but he did not mind making rather bad jokes; there is hope in that for some of us. I am afraid, though, that the details of that story are not quite certain. St. Bede simply hands it on as a tradition he has heard; and the earliest form of the story does not make the Angles slaves or boys at all; just grown-up Angles who happened to be visiting Rome. And with that, of course, all the point of their looking like Angels is lost. We think of the slave-boys looking very good and clean, like those cherubs with red cheeks and tow-coloured hair on the Christmas cards. I daresay really English boys, even then, would have looked rather grubby little brutes, and no one would have mistaken them for Angels. But the real point, you know, is quite unaffected by what they looked like. The real point is that they were citizens of Anglia, and St. Gregory said they ought to be fellow-citizens of the Angels. That was just like St. Gregory, and the age of St. Gregory. He objected to their Angularity. The Church had just begun to realize that she was outliving the Roman Empire, and saw in the spreading of the faith not a philosophy to be preached to the world, but a citizenship to be extended to it. It had been the boast of the Roman Empire that it made the most distant and most barbarous tribes into citizens of a single world-state:

> She (prouder boast than other conquerors knew)
> Gently the captives to her bosom drew;
> Mother, not mistress, made the thrall her kin,
> And 'neath her wing drew all the nations in.
> Orontes knows in Syria, Rhone in Gaul,
> One speech, one race, one governance for all:
> Whate'er is Earth, is Rome; Rome stands till Earth
>   shall fall.

St. Gregory, then, like the statesman he was, thinks of these Anglians not as ignorant people who need to be instructed, but as unhappy barbarians whose hearts must be conquered in order that a citizenship may be extended to them—the citizenship of the Angelic kingdom.

When we received the faith, we received it not (as other nations) like a microbe which we caught from our neighbours, nor as a bargain which we picked up from travelling pedlars, we were simply annexed to Rome by a single act of spiritual conquest. I do not say that there were not Christians wandering about in England before

St. Augustine came. I do not say that the Irish would not have converted us sooner or later even if the Italians had not been first. All I say is that as a matter of fact our conversion was a purely Roman affair. You will still, occasionally, read of Protestant fellow-countrymen of ours referring to the Catholic Church in England under the contemptuous title of 'the Italian Mission.' The name is meant, of course, to twit us with being foreigners, because during the penal times our priests were educated abroad. It is a delightful idea: you make the Mass high treason, and put a price on every priest's head, and so seminaries have to be built abroad, and priests have to come back from foreign centres if they want to preserve the old faith. And when they do come back, you greet them with shouts of: 'Oh, you beastly Italian.' Well, I am not considering here whether that is a very generous taunt, or a very intelligent one: the interesting point about it is, Who was the first to make it? It was made first by Archbishop Benson, father of Msgr. Hugh Benson. And what was he? Archbishop of Canterbury. And why Canterbury? Why that very one-horse, dead-and-alive place on the South-Eastern? Simply because St. Augustine, not being able to go on as far as London, had to wait about there for a time and so set up his See there. St. Augustine, a Roman envoy sent by the Pope to convert our country to the religion of the Church of Rome. And then an Archbishop of Canterbury describes the diocese of Westminster as an Italian Mission!

Well, we were founded from Rome; and all through the Middle Ages, in spite of the nuisance of living so far away from it, we were known for our loyalty to the Roman See.

In St. Gregory's time men were looking to the Church as the one abiding institution; it seemed to them that the break-up of earthly dominions and the shifting of nations which was taking place throughout Europe pointed to mere chaos ahead, unless hope lay in the Papacy. To-day there is the same break-up of great dominions; the same shifting of the limits of nationality. The world has altered its look since we learned our geography, and it has not got to the end of its alteration yet. In this new world men still look to the Catholic Church, and to Rome as the divinely-appointed centre of the Catholic Church, as the one abiding institution which will survive the new chaos. And we, without ceasing to be Angles (those of us who are Angles), will have to rally more than ever round the Holy See as the centre of our true citizenship, that Angelic citizenship which was St. Gregory's gift to us. We ought to be praying earnestly for the Holy Father. We ought to be praying for the conversion of those who, disheartened by the failure of civilization, are turning to the Church for guidance.

May the King of Angels bring us all to the fellowship of the heavenly citizens; to him be glory for ever and ever. Amen.

IV

St. Edward the Confessor

(*Preached at St. Edwards, Golders Green*)

For the hope of the wicked is as dust, which is blown away with the wind, and as a thin froth which is dispersed by the storm, and a smoke that is scattered abroad by the wind, and as the remembrance of a guest of one day that passeth by. But the just shall live for evermore, and their reward is with the Lord, and the care of them with the most High (Wis 5:15).

SOMETHING LIKE two months back there died, with the greatest publicity that can attend a death-bed, one of the most characteristic and one of the most successful figures of our time. A man of business, he had restricted himself to a single form of business—that journalism which sells to the public the news it wants to hear told and the views it wants to hear expressed. A man of political ambition, he contented himself with a single form of political activity—that journalism which praises or blames, and to the best of its power appoints or dismisses, parliaments and ministers of the Crown. Hewing his own way up the difficult path of public fame by the force of his native energy, he achieved a position of prominence almost unrivalled in our memory. True, it was not one of personal prominence; we did not often see his portrait or hear what manner of man he was: many whose thought he influenced from day to day did not even know his title. True again, it was a precarious power he exercised; for the newspaper proprietor, while he aspires to be the tyrant of public opinion, must in many ways stoop to be its slave. Yet within those limits he stood before the world a titanic figure; and when a banquet was given in his honour, a clergyman of the Established Church tactfully included his name among the blessings which he commemorated at grace. Did he do good in the world, or evil? Probably a good deal of both, and both alike accidentally, for he had no mission to preach, and no selfish cupidity to satisfy. Only one thing he asked, the power of an enormous publicity, and that wish was granted him: never, probably, has a man succeeded so utterly in that which he set before himself to accomplish. And then God required his soul of him, and he died.

He died, and they held a memorial service for him. They held a memorial service for him in Westminster Abbey, that strange mausoleum of nine hundred years of English history which is neither church nor cathedral, because it is too proud to be either. And as the great congregation that celebrated his obsequies reminded one another, to the plaintive pealing of the organ, that

> Time like an ever-rolling stream bears all its sons away;
> They fly forgotten, as a dream dies at the opening day,

how many of them gave a thought to the poignantly contrasted character of that English king who built the Abbey, and who still keeps in the Abbey his unhonoured shrine? That king, whose more than royal memory the universal Church celebrates at this time?

Let me give you in brief *his* biography. Born to a throne bequeathed to him by a line of strong men, whose vigorous qualities he was little likely to emulate, he was driven into exile at the age of ten years; it seemed that a fortunate catastrophe had robbed him of the terrors of royalty. Himself, patient under that exile, he declared that he would rather remain uncrowned than win a kingdom at the cost of blood. That hope was unrealized; he was restored with the goodwill of the Norman Duke, already England's rival and soon to be her invader. Very naturally, he took for his advisers and administrators men of the race that had befriended his exile. Insignificant in person (he was probably an albino) and lacking at least in his public policy the sterner qualities of mind, he became a puppet king in the hands of an unpopular clique, his mother's kinsmen. There was a revolt, and his Norman advisers fled the country; he became a puppet king once more, overshadowed this time by the figure of the great Saxon earl whose daughter he had taken to wife. Taken, rather, for his spouse: for they had no children, and it is constantly asserted that they never lived as man and wife. The one benefit he might have conferred upon his country, by leaving an heir in whose veins Norman and Saxon blood would mingle, he refused of his own choice. His kingdom, already pledged to the Normans, he now had to bequeath to a Saxon champion. Foreseeing clearly in his last moments the harvest of slaughter which was to be the reaping of his own peaceful reign, he died. He died, and thirty-six years later they found his body uncorrupted, and breathing the odour of sanctity.

What a record of failure! What a negation of all that the

politicians value, and all that the historians revere! Other Saints, other kings whose memory is venerated, have been no less ineffective in their lives, yet breathe some atmosphere of tragedy which endeared them to posterity. St. Peter Celestine was unequal to the task of government, but he signalized himself in history by resigning the triple tiara. Henry of Windsor was a weak man born in a distracted age, but the story of his murder rallied to him the sympathies of his people. Edward, no less incompetent in his lifetime than St. Peter Celestine or the sixth Henry, died crowned and died a natural death. One great thing he gave to his country, the Abbey Church of Westminster. And that church, with an absence of humour singular even among our fellow-countrymen, they have chosen to be the burial-place of England's great national heroes—not asking what creed they held or what life they lived, but only whether they achieved fame.

> Mortality, behold and Fear!
> What a change of flesh is here!
> Here they lie had realms and lands,
> Who now want strength to stir their hands,
> Where, from their pulpits sealed with dust,
> They preach, 'in greatness is no trust.'
> Here's an acre sown indeed
> With the richest, royallest seed
> That the earth did e'er suck in
> Since the first man died for sin.

Soldier, and statesman, and lawyer, they wait for the last trumpet, and the world's dissolution, and the great Assize. And amidst them all sleeps the poor weakling who graced so ill the throne of England, and they are stared

at by visitors, while he, the builder of the Abbey, is forgotten.

We know that there is another side to the picture, a
side to which historians, full of great world movements
and the fortunes of dynasties, pay scant attention. We
know that if he abstained from the use of marriage it was
because he hoped to win the palm of virginity. We know
that while Norman duke and Saxon earl forgot the poor
puppet who had served their turn and slipped through
their hands, the poor, better canonizers than earl or duke,
remembered the good king Edward as the man who had
remitted their taxes and lavished his own fortune upon
their needs. We know that in his lifetime men loved him
for his gentleness and kindness of heart, and that both in
life and death Almighty God ratified their judgement by
granting him miraculous favours. But for all his practical effect upon our history he might as well never have
lived, had better, perhaps, never have reigned. When we
venerate St. Edward, we venerate a failure.

We do so advisedly. Not because success in life neces-
sarily falls to the grasping and the unscrupulous, so that
success itself should be mistrusted by Christians as a sign
of rascality. Not that there have not been great Saints who
were also great kings, great statesmen, great warriors, St.
Oswald, St. Dunstan, St. Joan of Arc. But because we will
not let ourselves be blinded by the lure of worldly success so as to forget that the true statesmanship is exercised
in the council chamber, and the true warfare fought on
the battlefield of the human soul. Ask yourself which you
would rather have been, in life, of all those great dead who
lie in Westminster Abbey, and you will find it a difficult

question to answer: there is so much that dazzles, so much that captivates the imagination. Would you rather have written this, have painted that, have built that, have discovered that, have won this triumph or have carried that enactment—you can hardly say. But ask yourself which of those great dead you would rather be now, your body there, your soul far away—is there any Christian who would not ask to change places with the Confessor; who would not choose his resting-place, there to wait for the opening of the great Doomsday Book, in which nothing is recorded of men, but whether they meant good or evil, whether they loved or neglected God?

The hope of the wicked is as dust which is blown away . . . but the reward of the just is for evermore. All through this very beautiful passage in the Book of Wisdom the just man is the simpleton, the natural prey of designing enemies. They deride him, they make him a parable of reproach; they esteem his life madness and his end without honour. All the maxims of worldly prudence, all the sensible considerations, seem to be on their side. The best that can happen to him, the just man, is that he should be taken away, lest wickedness should alter his understanding, or deceit beguile his soul. He is not fit to fight the cunning of his age with its own weapons. And, by a defiant paradox, the book is called the Book of Wisdom! It is a deliberate paradox, for the word 'wise' in Scriptural language has often the sense of crafty; the Unjust Steward is commended because he acted wisely, and the children of this world in their generation are wiser than the children of light. But there is a wisdom which somehow these innocent, gullible, ineffective, open-handed simpletons have got hold of; while these smart, up-to-date, very much alive men of business have missed it. Now, which is right?

Our Divine Lord, quoting from the Psalms of David, has assured us that the meek shall possess the earth. Does that mean that meekness is one of those qualities which will gain men a brighter crown in the heavenly kingdom that is to come? It does, of course, but does it mean nothing more? Certainly in this, as in any other age of history, it does not seem as if it is the meek who carry off the world's prizes; go where you will, the advertisements of the mind-training systems and the correspondence colleges will cry out to you that life is a stern battle, that success is for the ambitious, and that the weakest goes to the wall. There is no room, it would seem, for the saintly albinos. Does Christianity, then, simply preach the survival of the unfittest, by promising us in heaven a reversal of all human values and a revision of all human judgements? And must it always be, in this world, the Godwins and the Harolds and the Williams who have the best time, make the best use of their opportunities?

The land of a certain rich man brought forth plenty of fruits. And he thought within himself, saying: What shall I do, because I have no room here to bestow my fruits? And he said: This will I do; I will pull down my barns, and will build greater, and into them I will gather all things that are grown to me and my goods. And I will say to my soul: Soul, thou hast much goods laid up for many years: take thy rest, eat, drink, make good cheer. But God said to him: Thou fool, this night do they require thy soul of thee. And whose shall those things be which thou hast provided? So is he that layeth up treasure for himself and is not rich towards God. In that telling, almost bitter parable, Our Divine Lord has shown us the fallacy of the successful life, not only from the point of view of the next world, but even in this. If the rich fool had not died then, do you think he would really have carried out his resolution of retiring from business? Not he. He would have gone on, as he had already gone on all those years, wearing himself out in the pursuit of a visionary contentment which he continually promised himself, yet could never rest to enjoy it. A record harvest? Why, then, he must build yet greater barns. And when the barns were built, he would have extended his farming operations so as to have more fruits to fill them with. He was a fool, because he became the slave of his own ambitions. Mind you, we are not told that he was wicked. We are not told that, like Dives, he neglected the poor, and went like Dives into the place of torment. No, we are only told that he was a fool; that his life was a wasted one. No doubt but his funeral sermon and his obituary notices called him a successful man; a pioneer of agriculture, and one who had revolutionized the old type of barn. But in the stillness of the night in which God spoke to him, he knew that he was a failure.

His was a selfish life; not all the lives the world calls successful are selfish lives. Many of those who sleep in King Edward's Abbey were devoted servants of their kind, who left the world better for their passing. But this is certain, that true satisfaction came to them and true success crowned them only so far as their ambitions were for a cause, not for a party, for others, not for themselves.

Man's happiness lies in devoting himself, his success in the offering he can make. And our Confessor was a successful man, yes, even in this world, because in his simple piety, in the unaffected generosity of his nature, he set himself to serve men about him by easing their burdens, by relieving their necessities, by confirming them in their allegiance to the faith. Great opportunities passed him by, and he never marked them; he might have altered the dynastic history of England, have left us different manners and a different political constitution, if he had been other than he was. Instead, he left all these things to God's Providence; and God's Providence, using the ambitions of human agents as its puppets, moulded our history beyond man's expectation. And what do they mean to us now, those human agents? Mere names in the history book, mere stiff, attitudinizing figures on the Bayeux Tapestry, they have become part of a past hardly less remote to us than legend. As dust which is blown away with the wind, and as a thin froth that is dispersed by the storm, and a smoke that is scattered abroad by the wind, and as the remembrance of a guest of one day that passeth by. The Conqueror, who diverted the stream of history, went to his grave disappointed and lies there a historical memory. The Confessor, whose ambitions could be satisfied by finding a poor man his dinner, saw no corruption in death, and lives, the patron of his fellow-countrymen.

One only task he set before himself that had any external magnificence about it, and that was characteristic of him. It was no fortress, no royal palace, no court of justice that he planned: the House of God lay waste, and he must rebuild it. And, as if it were a symbol of the life he lived, built together from little acts of kindness and little sacrifices of self, stone by stone and arch by arch rose the Abbey Church of Westminster, which for all the additions and the restorations that have altered it in the course of the centuries, we still call his church. The building was actually completed about a week before his death: and, if pride held any place in his gentle character, he must have felt proud to think that he had left one lasting memorial; that while his monks continued their daily round of prayer, the last of the dynasty of Egbert would not be forgotten.

And yet, though his Abbey still stands, and even his shrine was protected—ironically enough, by the shadow of royalty—from desecration, the liturgy of the Church he loved so well is no more celebrated in the house he built for it. Westminster, with all the other monuments of our Catholic antiquity, has passed into other hands and hears strange doctrines preached. It has remained for devoted men in the last two generations to replace, as best they could with the resources they had at their disposal, that loss suffered by religion. And among the churches that have thus been raised, not the least remarkable for its splendid proportions and its commanding site is this church in which we claim his patronage to-day. And this church, too, will perpetuate the memory of a founder, in whom those who knew him at all could not but discern the signs of a saintly character. Here was another unsuccessful life, as the world judges success—a life in which a spirit of indomitable energy was long thwarted in its activities and too soon cut off by a discipline of terrible and (the world would say) meaningless suffering. You have done well to commemorate him at its high altar; for its history is bound up with his; and so long as the Holy Sacrifice is offered in this place, it should be offered with grateful memory of the prayers and the cruel mortifications which Father Bendon used to offer for his parish and his people.

Their reward is with the Lord, and the care of them with the most High. May the prayers of Our Blessed Lady, and St. Edward our patron, and all the Saints of God bring us safely from this world of humiliation and of suffering into the kingdom of the just.

V

St. Anselm

(*Preached at St. Anselm and St. Cecilia's, Kingsway*)

And I said: Woe is me, because I have held my peace, because I am a man of unclean lips, and I dwell in the midst of a people that hath unclean lips, and I have seen with my eyes the King, the Lord of hosts (Is 6:5).

I T IS a curious thing what a lot of coincidences there are in history. Three Archbishops of Canterbury, and only three, between the Norman Conquest and the time of England's apostasy, have been raised to the altars of the Church; St. Thomas, the patron of all our secular clergy, your patron St. Anselm, and my patron St. Edmund. Each of those three men spent a significant part of his time of office in exile overseas. They belonged, respectively, to the reigns of Henry I, Henry II, and Henry III. The attitude of the reigning sovereign was, in each case, the cause of the Saint's difficulties and of his consequent merits—a gloomy omen for the day when an eighth Henry should arise, and a time-server be found enthroned at Lambeth.

And there is a singular sort of mathematical progression, I think, about the three characters if you consider them side by side. St. Edmund was made Archbishop because he was a Saint and everybody knew it. St. Thomas was made Archbishop because he was the last person you would have expected to become a Saint—you might almost as well have expected it of Thomas Cromwell, or of Thomas Cranmer. St. Edmund's temperament produces few Archbishops but many Saints, St. Thomas' few Saints but many Archbishops. St. Edmund would have been a far happier man if he had never worn a mitre; his archbishopric was only an addition to his long series of mortifications. St. Thomas, humanly speaking, only learned to develop his Sainthood as the result of being made Archbishop; his archbishopric was the occasion of his self-realization. St. Edmund was a Saint first and an Archbishop afterwards; he learned to be great in spite of being good. With St. Thomas, in order of time, the process was reversed; he learned to be good in spite of being great. To put it roughly, and merely from the human point of view, you may say that St. Edmund probably would not have become Archbishop if he had not been a Saint, and St. Thomas would not have become a Saint if he had not been Archbishop.

In your holy patron St. Anselm these opposing characteristics are curiously reconciled. When he first set foot in our country you may say that he already had all St. Edmund's qualifications for heaven, and all St. Thomas' qualifications for Lambeth. Take away his prelacy, and you still leave a character comparable with that of St. Edward the Confessor. Take away his saintliness, and you still leave a career that rivals the career of Lanfranc. This was the man who, with some misgiving, came over to visit a sick friend in England at a time when the archbishopric of Canterbury had long been left vacant, so that King William Rufus and his creatures might enjoy the sequestrated revenues of the See. You will read in Dean

Church's life of St. Anselm how at Christmas, 1092, the clergy were allowed to pray for a remedy for the misfortunes of the Church. You will read on the next page how, early in 1093 (which means, if you come to think of it, about a fortnight later) King William fell sick and was evidently at the point of death. The Anglican biographer does not seem to connect the two events even by way of coincidence: fortunately for himself, the Norman king was more prompt in seeing the point of the situation. He promised amendment and restitution of every possible kind, and sent for Anselm at once as the obvious person to be elected Archbishop.

And then began a scene which has been enacted with various results a thousand times in the history of sanctity, but seldom with so much publicity or so much dramatic interest as in St. Anselm's case. When you try to make a Saint accept a bishopric, it is like trying to make a child take medicine: the result is a perfect fury of dissent. Calculation, argument, even personal dignity are thrown to the winds; the Saint like the child simply sticks to his point and says: 'I won't, I won't, I WON'T.' In this case not merely the ordinary considerations but the whole welfare of a long-widowed Church and, as seemed probable, the life of a notorious sinner were depending upon St. Anselm's acceptance, and he simply refused. 'A great post like the archbishopric,' writes Dean Church, 'may have had irresistible terrors, overwhelming all its attractions or temptations, to a religious mind and conscience in the eleventh century'—a comment that speaks better for the courage of eleventh-century bishops than for the sense of humour of nineteenth-century deans. Anyhow, it was only by the use of physical force that they dragged the Saint to the King's bedside; and there, pressing the crozier against the knuckles that would not open so as to hold it, they elected the Archbishop of Canterbury.

St. Anselm is, from many points of view, a famous man, and stood out like a giant among his contemporaries. Yet the work he did was not final, for no human work is final. He was a monastic reformer, but others carried monastic reform further after his death. He was an intrepid champion of the Church against the Crown; and that is the same thing as to say that he defended the prerogatives of St. Peter with a firmness which no glosses of the historian can conceal: but even here his work had to be done over again by St. Thomas à Becket. He was a philosopher and a theologian, yet to-day his theological views are generally quoted in order to be refuted, and his most famous exploit in philosophy, the ontological proof of the existence of God, is not only discredited but has, according to some, the dubious credit of being the parent of modern idealism. So I will not apologize for leaving out these considerations—the sort of considerations you get in an obituary notice—and asking you to concentrate your attention on the scene I was describing just now, and to consider with me why it was that the Saints, why it was that St. Anselm, always began by refusing, and sometimes succeeded in refusing altogether, the offer of ecclesiastical preferment?

Was it because the Saints were incompetent in the managing of affairs, and knew it? That might have been true in some cases, but it certainly was not in St. Anselm's; he had already given good proof of his competency by being

Abbot of a large monastery—running a monastery is not always a sinecure. Or was it that they thought they were incompetent although they were not? Surely, if that had been all, obedience should have triumphed over humility, and they should have been content to acquiesce in the estimate others had formed of their worth. Or were they simply afraid that they would not get enough time to say their prayers? But St. Anselm was a very busy man already. Or were they afraid of the temptation to worldliness, to love of money, to subservience which high office brings with it? But they must have known that other candidates were, humanly speaking, much more likely to succumb to those temptations than themselves: the good man, Plato tells us, accepts office in the State not for any advantage he gets from it, but because he fears the possibility of worse men than himself attaining to office instead. Or was it that they disliked all the pomp and fuss of it? But they could keep their secret intention pure. All those ordinary reasons which would make it very bad for you or me to be made a bishop were alleged by the Saints as excuses, but surely only as excuses. There must be some deeper reason to explain this phenomenon that is always meeting us in hagiography, from St. Celestine resigning the triple tiara to the Curé d'Ars running away like a schoolboy from the little French parish where everybody idolized him.

It is not that the Saint has become unpractical, like the philosopher: the philosopher blinks because he has come out of the darkness of his study into the light of common things; the Saint blinks because he has come out of the light of his oratory into the darkness of the world. He has been with God; and in seeing, as we do not see, the greatness of God, he has seen, as we do not see, his own smallness. It is not that he exaggerates his smallness; he is not like the horse, which shies (so clever people tell us) because its eyes are focused wrong and it sees everything around it twice as big as it really is. No, the Saint has got the true perspective, and we the false. Woe is me, because I have held my peace—in the solitude of prayer he has learned his own miserable helplessness. I am a man of unclean lips, and dwell in the midst of a people of unclean lips—he has no illusion, you see, about his neighbours being to any great extent better than himself. And I have seen with my eyes the King, the Lord of Hosts—that is it. To the man who has once seen himself as he looks in comparison with God, all worldly preferment, not because it is too high or because it is too low a sphere for his attainments, not because others seem more competent to fill the post, not because it entails labour or responsibility, but simply because it must in some measure make him the recipient of worldly homage and give him honour in the sight of men, is an anomaly not to be thought of, a miscarriage of justice to be avoided at all costs.

It is not a question of one man being more or being less worthy than another, the plain fact is, if you have only got your eyes focused right, that any job is too big for any of us, because all worldly station involves the bestowing of some credit, and bestowing it where in truth credit is not due. Modesty is quite a different thing from humility. It is a very attractive thing, modesty, even where it is something of an affectation. The boy, for example, who got the D.S.O. almost immediately after leaving school, and when we asked him what he was doing when he got it could only reply: 'Oh, I don't know, fooling round some-where, I suppose'—that is modesty. There is a great deal of modesty going about; it is fashionable, and the lack of it stamps you with vulgarity—a lot of modesty, but very little humility. For modesty is only the disinclination to hear our own praises sounded above those of other men; by humility man learns that simply because he is man he is nothing. Of such humility the Queen of Heaven her-self could leave us an example; let us make it the sub-ject of our prayer on St. Anselm's festival. We can find excuses for ourselves when we do not rival the Saints in their heroic exercise of other virtues, but it is not so with their humility. For in proportion as we are less than they, with all the more justice can it be claimed of us that we should be humble.

And remember, this Christian humility does not unfit a man for great deeds. A critic of St. Edmund might say of his *Nolo episcopari*: 'Well, perhaps after all he was right; perhaps a more unscrupulous man would have made a more successful job of the archbishopric in his day.' But St. Anselm does not even leave room for the worldly point of view. He knew, in his humility, that neither he nor any other man living was worthy of the crozier that was pressed against his clenched fingers, but, once clasped, it was clasped in a grip of iron. We must not be afraid, then, of the meditation of our own littleness: it could not dim the lustre of Anselm's earthly fame, yet made his coronal in heaven shine, who knows how much brighter? May his prayers protect the Church he laboured in life to defend, still bringing back stubborn hearts to the allegiance of the Holy See: his prayers win for each one of us the grace he most needs, to God's glory and our eternal salvation.

VI

St. Dominic

(Preached at St. Dominic's, Haverstock Hill)

Ye are the salt of the earth. But if the salt lose its savour,
wherewith shall it be salted? (Matt 5:13).

TWO MEN, at the beginning of the thirteenth century,
were raised up by God to season his Church, that
seemed in danger of perishing through its own corruption. They were both comparatively short-lived. God will
be glorified, now in a short lifetime, now in the fullness
of years; St. John Vianney, whom we celebrate on Thursday, died worn out with his labours at the age of seventy-
three; St. Laurence, whom we celebrate on Friday, was
cut down by persecution during his diaconate. If you add
the ages of St. Francis and St. Dominic together, they do
not cover a full century. And the career of St. Dominic is
particularly remarkable, because he did not find out what
his life's work was to be until he was thirty-five years old,
with only sixteen more years to live. That short time suf-
ficed for doing the special thing God had called him to
do; for meeting a particular situation, and warding off a
particular danger from the gates of Christendom. If you
will bear with me, I will sketch very briefly—at the risk
of repeating things you may have heard yesterday and the
day before—what that situation, what that danger was.

Two important heresies at that time threatened the peace, and perhaps the life of the Church; the Waldensian and the Albigensian heresies. The Waldenses, of whom a remnant still remains in Italy, seem to have been among the most harmless of the sects; erring through their simpleness rather than through any constructive malice. Scandalized by the riches of the higher clergy, by the sight of so many priests living unpriestly lives, they formed themselves into a little Protestant community before the time of Protestantism was yet come. They lived in poverty, they studied and translated the Bible, they refused, like the Anabaptists and the Quakers after them, to bind themselves by any form of oath. Their main false doctrine was that a priest living in mortal sin was no priest at all; and they thought to replace the ministry of the ordained clergy by a kind of lay ministry of their own. They were, if such a phrase may be used, Noncomformists rather than heretics; and it is possible that, if they had not been involved in the fate of less worthy neighbours, they would have been treated by the Church with leniency, and returned gradually to her communion.

But the Albigenses, who resembled them outwardly, because they too made a parade of great simplicity and innocence, were the revival or the continuation of a very old and very dangerous heresy; that Manichean heresy which attracted, for a time, the restless genius of St. Augustine. In order to account for the existence of the evil in the world, the Manichean maintains a total divorce between matter and spirit, believing that matter is of its nature evil, and owes its existence not to the Providence of God but to the interference of a malign spirit. Accordingly, he rejects the doctrine of the Incarnation, which degrades, to his mind, the spiritual nature of the Godhead. The more fully initiated of the sect, who called themselves the Perfect, repudiated altogether the use of marriage, and abstained, in their diet, from all animal life and whatever owed its origin to animal life. They were the declared enemies of Christendom, and, patronized as they were by the Count of Toulouse, threatened to supersede it altogether in the southern districts of France.

We remember St. Dominic and his order, in the first instance, for the intellectual protest which they opposed to that sinister outbreak of Oriental philosophy in the heart of Western Christendom. Heresies, after all, have their place in the elucidation of religious truth. The fine flower of Christian scholarship is fertilized, you may say, by the decaying corpse of false doctrine. Or perhaps you may say with greater accuracy that Christian theology has at all times been a reaction to the assaults of heresy, just as a living organism will develop a protective shell there, where a hostile stimulus from without has made itself felt. When the germs of the Manichean heresy sought to find a lodgement in the healthy body of Christendom, the reaction of that healthy body was the great Dominican tradition of learning. It developed, we may well believe, beyond the Saint's own hopes. Almost at the moment of his death another Saint was being born to carry on his work; St. Thomas, destined like Eliseus to have a double portion of his Master's spirit. Who shall say what we owe to that Providential impetus which the Manichean peril gave to Christian thought? Just as a healthy body may gain immunity from a disease by being inoculated with a mild form of it, so Christian thought was immunized against the false doctrines which threatened to destroy it, three centuries later, by its inoculation with the dying germs of Orientalism which it had encountered, and triumphed over, at Toulouse.

That intellectual protest we associate especially with the Dominican order, because it is more individually, more characteristically theirs. The sons of St. Francis only entered the vineyard of scholarship as late-comers, by a happy deflection from their original design. But meanwhile, let us not forget that the coming of the Friars was a moral protest too; and in that moral protest the sons of St. Dominic from the first took, and were meant to take, their full part; Cherubim and Seraphim must hymn together the dazzling holiness of God. Those were times, it is sad to say it, in which the Church seemed to have lost the salt wherewith Christ had commissioned it to season the world. The great St. Bernard was dead; and the monastic orders, even at their best, were too remote from the world to affect powerfully the standard of Christian living. There were crying abuses; and, whereas the Albigensians, a purely destructive movement, deserve little of our sympathy, the poor Waldenses could at least claim that they had reason for the disaffection which made them the antagonists of the Church. An intellectual heresy can be met by the weapons of the intellect; a moral protest, such as that of the Waldenses, can only be met by a rival moral protest within the Church itself. Just as the tide of the Reformation was stemmed, not merely by polemical writing and preaching, but by the great spiritual renewal which was accomplished throughout Europe by the Saints of the sixteenth century, so three hundred years earlier it was not only the learning of the Friars, but their poverty, their chastity, the simplicity of their lives and manners, that saved Europe for the faith.

Reverend Fathers, the times in which we live, seven hundred years removed from those days of persecution and terror, still need the intellectual protest, still need the moral. The old difficulty of reconciling God's omnipotence with his benevolence still presses upon us; and to-day, instead of trying to save the one at the expense of the other, like the medieval heretics, men are driven, by that apparent inconsistency, to deny his very existence. It is to you, with the old weapons in your hands, that we look for the solving of these difficulties as of those; like King David, when he found once more the sword with which he slew the giant in the valley of the terebinth, 'there is none like that' we say, 'give it me.' But while we call upon you as scholars for an intellectual protest against the tendencies of the age, we call upon you as Friars for a moral protest as well. For the times are evil; and the world's mind would not have travelled so far from God if its heart had not travelled far from God first.

We heard much lately in the newspapers—not so much quite lately, for the newspapers tire of their fancies quickly —about a new religious movement in the Protestant world around us which was to have prodigious effects in bringing men back to the service of God. It has much in common with earlier revivalist movements; and in one point at least it may well remind us of the Waldenses, about whom we were speaking just now. The Waldenses, as I was saying, distrusted the ministrations of an ordained clergy; every good man, they held, in so far as he is a good man, is a priest. Just so these new teachers have revived the idea of confession; but their confessions are made, not to an ordained minister of whatever denomination, but to one another—to the friends in whose goodwill and spiritual insight they can trust. I do not know whether this particular movement is destined to fulfil the hopes of its promoters; but of this at least I feel certain, that either this or some similar reaction will begin, before long, to stem the tide of demoralization which has so long closed in upon our society. Grace, like nature, abhors a vacuum; and any public neglect of God and of the soul's needs will be followed, before long, by a return. Are we to suffer our fellow-countrymen to take refuge once more in the half-truths of a revived Protestantism, instead of learning to find peace where true peace can alone be found, in the bosom of the Catholic Church?

We shall suffer them to do that, unless we can oppose to the revived spirit of Protestantism a revived spirit of Catholicism. We Catholics want more simplicity, more contentment with plain living and with common things, more unworldliness about money and social position, more daily trust in Providence, more honesty of speech, more kindliness towards our fellow-men; we want to get away from a great deal of that complexity, that sophistication, that worship of good form, into which the influence of our modern surroundings has led us. We want to restore, somehow, not the outward conditions, but the moral attitude which belonged to the medieval world. It is to the mendicant orders, to you not less than to the Franciscans, that we must look if we are to revive that spirit of gaiety which goes with poverty, that open-hearted acceptance of the world which belongs only to those who have learned to despise it. Your continuous tradition must link us with our past, if we are to find refuge from this over-mechanized, over-commercialized age; like a shaft bringing the fresh airs of the sea into a Tube station. Persuade us that the Catholic religion is something more than a mere label, a mere favour that a man can wear on his sleeve; that it is a life, and an interpretation of life; an attitude towards our daily tasks, as well as an attitude towards God.

We expect of you that to-day, as seven hundred years ago, you should leaven human thought, by justifying the ways of God to men; by asserting the truth of our Lord's Incarnation, and vindicating the honour of his Blessed Mother. We expect of you also that to-day, as seven hundred years ago, you should leaven human society, by showing us in your own lives, and in the lives of that great Third Order which derives its inspiration from you, the grand simplicity of former times. So will men learn to find, in the Catholic Church, the key to their disillusionment, and the remedy for their despairs; learning will not do that, argument will not do that. May the prayers of your holy patron, raised so long ago by an infallible oracle to the altars of the Church, win such grace for you and for us; may the bewildered minds of our non-Catholic fellow-countrymen be led back, more and more, through the Dominicans to Dominic, and through Dominic to Christ.

VII

St. Edmund of Abingdon

(Preached at St. Edmund's, Ware)

And the priest said: Lo, here is the sword of Goliath the Philistine, whom thou slewest in the valley of the terebinth. . . . If thou wilt take this, take it, for there is no other but this. And David said: There is none like that; give it me (1 Kings 21:9).

WE HAVE no means of knowing what was the age of David when this interview took place. Certainly he was married, and had occupied an important military position; we may imagine him, perhaps, as nearing thirty. The bitter jealousy of King Saul, the master whom he had served so faithfully, had driven him to take refuge as an outlaw among the hills. On his way he visits the priests at Nobe, who supply him and his followers with bread for their journey. Then—it seems a poor chance, but he asks if they have a sword there; he has come out unarmed. And they tell him: Yes, there is one sword, the sword of Goliath the Philistine, the giant whom David himself slew, and dedicated the sword he had plundered from his body in the tabernacle of God.

As the priest is talking, David's mind travels back over the years, ten years perhaps, and he sees the valley of the terebinth as if it were yesterday. He sees himself as a boy, rather tired and hot after his journey from Bethlehem—

he had been bringing presents from his father to his three
soldier brothers, a bushel of corn, and ten loaves of bread,
and ten small cheeses for their commanding officer, with
father's compliments. To and fro along the valley strides
the gigantic figure of the Philistine, taunting the armies of
Israel and challenging them to provide a champion who
will meet him in single combat. David remembers how
he expected his brothers to be pleased with their ham-
per from home, and how disappointed he was at the very
elder-brotherly greeting of the eldest, Eliab: 'Why camest
thou hither? And why didst thou leave those few sheep in
the desert? I know thy pride, and the wickedness of thy
heart, that thou art come down to see the battle.' So unfair
of him—and besides, David *had* wanted to see the battle
rather. And then the sudden resolve, to ask if he might accept the giant's challenge—that heroic resolution, with
just a faint tinge of anxiety to get even with Eliab. It
felt rather frightening at first, walking down the valley to
meet the boaster—and then he was kneeling down by the
brook side, while he picked up five pebbles just the shape
he wanted; and then the confidence he felt as the sling
whirled round his head, and the stone flew dead straight,
and hit his enemy full in the forehead, so that he lay there
stunned. Quick! no time to be lost; weaponless himself,
he takes out the giant's sword and cuts off the monstrous
head with it. And then, a confused memory, the stir and
the cry as the men of Israel went out to battle. Yes, he
has seen many engagements since then; many a sword
has broken in his victorious hand, but . . . the sword he
took from Goliath, what could bring better omens for
his present journey? There is none like that; give it me!

Let me give you another picture for comparison—one, perhaps, with which you are more familiar; St. Edmund on board ship, looking back at the cliffs of Dover for the last time. He, too, is going into exile, though it be voluntary exile; he, too, is hated and thwarted by the king for whom he has done so much, for whom he would have done so much more. And to him too, surely, comes a picture of the past; only he needs a longer retrospect; it is nearly fifty years now since he first made that Channel crossing. He sees himself as a boy of fifteen or thereabouts, tremendously excited at the prospect of going to study at Paris. The sea itself was a stranger to him: he knew the Thames where it sweeps down nobly from Oxford to Abingdon, or where it hastens past the ferry at Bablockhythe; but the beauty and mystery of the ships and the magic of the sea—that was all a new experience. And probably, so wayward is memory in the associations she brings together, he connects that experience with the first time he wore a hair-shirt, his mother's parting gift. Smile at the picture if you will, but do not laugh at the symbol; he was going to the worldliest city of all time, and he was to keep himself unspotted from the world. That love of Christ and his Blessed Mother which he had learned at Oxford were to be put to a severer test now. Since then, St. Edmund has met the world at a hundred different angles in the course of his busy life, has done heroic penance, has inflicted cruel mortification on himself. But those first impressions of his boyhood, which the hair-shirt symbolizes, are still his formative impressions; the religion of his boyhood is still, to him, the giant's sword—there is none like that, give it me.

Will you place yourself, you who are an Old Edmundian, in some such position of retrospect, and let
your mind focus itself upon some incident, some impression, some crisis of your school time? Not on the common memories which you will be talking over later in the
day, about the rules which you broke, and the professors
whose lives you made uncomfortable: dig deeper, and
bring to light some aspect of your boyhood which you
have never discussed, except perhaps in the confessional.
The moment, it may be, or the period at which you realized and accepted your vocation to the priesthood. Hitherto, you had taken it for granted you were to be a priest;
then the awkward age came, and with it difficulties, temptations; you had to fight your way through, perhaps with
the advice of others, perhaps with the light God gave in
answer to your prayer. Or, not aspiring to the priesthood,
you nevertheless met on this field the first onslaught of
spiritual difficulties; doubts, temptations, falls into sin,
what you will. Hitherto, Confessions and Communions
had been scarcely more than a matter of routine; now
you had an enemy to face, perhaps to dislodge, and you
paused a little longer over your prayers in front of the
statue or the shrine. Try to recapture some such experience, and from it take heart for whatever needs, whatever dangers you experience now. The love of Christ and
of his Blessed Mother you learned here; the sword you
killed the giant with. Say to yourself: There is none like
that; give it me.

Meanwhile, may I address myself to present Edmundi-
ans, in so far as I still claim their attention? You have
been born into an age of decision for the world and

for the Catholic Church. Before our very eyes the half-faiths and the false Christianities which the Reformation brought with it are crumbling away. The number of their adherents is steadily diminishing, and even those who do profess to adhere to them are more and more abandoning belief in the Bible, belief in revelation, belief in the Sacraments, belief in a world of rewards and punishments hereafter. And it is not only their beliefs but their moral standards that are disappearing. Especially the sanctity of marriage is being profaned; divorce is treated as a natural occurrence; no age before ours has so openly and so flagrantly set at nought the ordinance of God. And, while Protestantism crumbles away, the Catholic Church is winning back lost ground. We Catholics, in our effort to convert England, are not like furniture removers, paid by the hour, slowly and gingerly piling things on to a van. We are like men fighting a fire, desperately keeping at bay, here and there, the flames of unbelief and of social disorder, while we hurriedly rescue all that we have time to rescue. The fire will get ahead of us if we stop to contemplate our work.

In such an age, to aspire to the priesthood is not to aspire to comforts or to earthly rewards. You do not want to be a priest who simply does his job and knows his rubrics and hopes to pay off a bit of the parish debt. You want to be an ambassador from God to men, ready to take every opening, to follow up every trail, where there is a human conscience to be enlightened or a lost soul to be won back. You want to love souls; if you do not love souls, you will be hard put to it, in a world of so many temptations, to save your own.

And even if the priesthood has no place in your ambitions, you must still want to leave St. Edmund's not as a
Catholic merely, but as a fighting Catholic and a working
Catholic. It is possible nowadays, thank God, for laymen
to take a direct and public part in spreading the faith. But
even apart from that, we Catholics do not live, as our
grandfathers used to live, in a sort of water-tight com-
partment, separated from the world around us. We mix
freely with Protestant neighbours, and either we shall influence them or they us. If we are not strongly fortified
in the practice of religion, their unbelief will tell upon
our faith, their low standard of morality will infect and
degrade our consciences. It is becoming a clear issue in
our day, the Church or nothing. Do you remember what
the priest said to David about the giant's sword? 'If thou
wilt take this, take it; for there is none other but this.'
So it is with the religion you are taught here: there is
none other but this. The doctrines which you are taught
in apologetics or Christian doctrine class are not a sort
of continuation of the gender rhymes; the practices of
piety in which you are encouraged are not a tiresome
regulation made for you by house masters. They are the
world's last hope, which is committed to your keeping.
They are the giant's sword, with which you now face the
temptations of boyhood, with which you will face later
the temptations of manhood. If thou wilt take this, take
it, for there is none other than this.

David was an outlaw in his own country; you, too, if
you are faithful Catholics, still more if you are preaching the Catholic religion, will be outlaws to some extent
in the world of to-day, a world which tends more and

more to banish religion from its speech and its thought. Other schools have other traditions—this one has bred great soldiers, this has been a nursery of poets, there the civic virtues are practised and extolled. Our tradition is a different one, and in these days, I think, a more important one. We are a college of outlaws; those who have gone out from us were men who could set their face against the false standards of the world they lived in, who could stem the current of their times instead of being carried away with it. The names which we record here, with honour and with gratitude, are not those of men whom the world recognized, men who ruled empires or moulded the thought of their day, but those of exiles condemned as traitors, men who loved England too well to leave England what it was. The College has seen many changes, and may see more, but one thing remains constant about our tradition, that the man who is ready to let the world dictate its beliefs to him is a bad Edmundian.

He at least would tell us so, whose festival we keep, whose relics we venerate here. He would tell us that even in a world avowedly Catholic, a world obedient in every outward observance to the discipline of our holy faith, the widest learning, the most cloistered humility, the most single-hearted sincerity of purpose are no protection against hatred, and calumny, and misunderstanding. He has loved justice and hated iniquity, *therefore* he dies in exile—the grim irony of that word 'therefore' should be the Edmundian's armour against the world. He lives and dies an exile who will not take the world at its own valuation, who despises its folly and protests against its wrongs. Even if there were no hereafter to reward us, could we doubt where the man's part lies, which standard beckons us to more adventure, the world's standard or Christ's? But we must not face that battle in blind confidence; we must learn to hold and to wield our boyhood's sword, the religion of the Catholic Church. If thou wilt take this, take it, for there is none other than this. And he said: There is none like that; give it me.

VIII

St. Albert the Great

Every scribe instructed in the kingdom of heaven is like to a man that is a householder, who bringeth forth out of his treasure new things and old (Matt 13:52).

M Y TEXT is one of those which we are accustomed to carry in our heads without remembering the occasion upon which the utterance was made, and, partly for that reason, to hesitate about the precise meaning we should attach to it. It comes, actually, at the end of that great chapter, his thirteenth, in which St. Matthew has collected for us seven of our Lord's parables, six of which, if not all seven, deal with the growth of his kingdom, the Church; the sower, the cockle among the wheat, the mustard seed, the leaven, the hidden treasure, the merchant seeking pearls, the net cast into the sea. And four are particularly concerned to point out to our Lord's hearers that his kingdom was not, as some of them imagined, to be a clean sweep of all that went before it, a complete break-away from all human experience. It was not to be a millennium, in which all sin and suffering would have disappeared; those who were partakers of it would not be all perfect souls, already confirmed in goodness and destined for eternal life. No, the new kingdom or *ecclesia* of Christ was to be in some ways like the old *ecclesia*, the

old congregation of the Jews. There would still be tares
among the wheat, worthless fish amongst the catch, side
by side with the others. Our Lord, therefore, is not exactly creating a new thing in the world when he lays the
foundations of his Church; in a sense he is only reconsti-
tuting, on a new basis and with more extended possibilities, the old *ecclesia* of the Jews which he called to himself
so long ago. Do the apostles understand that? They do?
Good, then they are scribes instructed in the kingdom
of heaven; they see that every new thing in human history is built against the background of some older thing
which went before it. As the picture gallery of some great
house preserves the memory of its ancestry, tracing down
to the latest instance the persistence of the same characteristics, and linking up the present with the past; so the
greatest institutions of the world are those which combine something ancient with something new. And among
these, even the Catholic Church.

It is a human weakness of ours to be always crying
out for complete novelty, an entire disseverance from our
past. Our old traditions have become so dusty with neglect, so rusted with abuse, that we are for casting them
on the scrap-heap and forgetting that they ever existed.
The Church conserves; she bears traces still of the Jewish
atmosphere in which she was cradled; traces, too, of the
old heathen civilization which she conquered. And in her
own history it is the same; nothing is altogether forgotten; every age of Christianity recalls the lineaments of an
earlier time. People think of her as if she kept a lumber-
room; it is not so; hers is a treasure-house from which

she can bring forth when they are needed things old as well as new.

It is not difficult to see how all this applies to the history of the thirteenth century, and the reinstatement of Aristotle's philosophy by St. Albert and St. Thomas. The first instinct of Christendom had been to neglect and to disparage the pagan authors, whose works were so saturated with allusions to an idolatrous worship. St. Jerome was afraid of being too good a Ciceronian to be a Christian; and St. Augustine was ashamed of having been moved to tears by the story of the Aeneid. Buried away in libraries, the works of the ancients slept on; there is no clear proof that the great library of Alexandria, for instance, suffered much from Christian hands. But the libraries had been collected in the East, and when the East passed under the dominion of Islam, Islam became, for better or worse, the world's librarian. So it was that when Aristotle returned to Europe he returned in Oriental guise, translated and interpreted by the sectaries of the False Prophet. His works were not only dusty with the neglect of centuries, they were corroded with the rust of heretical contamination. Is it wonderful that the Christian world mistrusted their influence? You have to imagine, if you seek for a modern parallel, a situation in which all the available scientific literature of the world should be in the hands of Soviet Russia, and accessible only in the form of editions scrawled over with Bolshevist comment. It was a heroic adventure, only made possible through the guidance of the Holy Spirit when the theologians of a new order, which still had its reputation for orthodoxy to establish, took upon themselves to make a niche for Aristotle in the ante-chambers of Christian thought. The old weapon, soiled and rusty, useless, you would have thought—but there were men ready to scour and polish it, and make use of it, an instrument as keen as ever, for the confuting of false doctrine and the systematization of knowledge.

New things and old—St. Albert, as a scribe instructed in the Kingdom of Heaven, realized perhaps more than most men of his day that the secular sciences had great advances still to make, and that there must be room for new discoveries in any philosophy which was to express fully the thought of mankind. It was an age unfriendly to research for many reasons. The best brains were either devoted to practical administration in the world, or to theological studies in the cloister; the tools of science, though they had already been dreamt of, had not yet been forged; above all, printing had not yet appeared, with all its opportunities for garnering the fruit of human speculation. And the men of to-day will speak in contemptuous terms of the medieval world, as one in which research made no progress; they forget the difficulties which I have just mentioned; they forget also that St. Albert was characteristic of his period no less than St. Thomas. And St. Albert certainly had the build of mind which goes to make the research worker. If he had enjoyed more leisure from controversy and from the cares of administration, he would be remembered, as Roger Bacon is remembered, as part of that false dawn of science which went before the Renaissance; and he would be honoured to-day for activities which he himself would have been the last to think important. But they are important, for this reason if for no other—they prove that the Middle Ages, in taking over Aristotle as their master, did not suppose he had said the last word on every possible subject of discussion. St. Albert was too good an Aristotelian to think that Aristotle must be always right; he would imitate his master, not merely by borrowing opinions from him, but by instituting original research as he did.

To-day, perhaps more than ever before, the world is eager to make a clean sweep of its past. The war has driven a deep furrow across human experience, separating all that went before it from all that has come and that is to come after it, hardly with less of decisiveness than the Flood in earlier civilizations, than the Christian era in later times. Because we are in a mess with our economics, because Russia has shewn the way to infidelity, because Europe is feeling after a new solidarity, this post-War world feels a different world to us elder people, and our juniors are not slow to rub it in. They talk, they write, as if the world of Einstein and Jeans and Rutherford and Eddington were a world re-born; as if every earlier guess after the truth were now superseded or exploded; as if, for the first time, we had begun to know. In such ears, what use to celebrate the praises of St. Albert? The very name sounds worse than medieval; it sounds Victorian.

That is the secret of the modern world's antipathy towards the Christian religion, and towards the Catholic Church in particular. They hate it not because it is something arrogant, not because it is something uncomfortable, not because it is something foreign, but because it is something out of date. They know that it will always bring new things and old out of its treasure-house, will not consent to the modern worship of the modern. And they know that there is strength in this deeply rooted tradition which can yet absorb, as it has absorbed all through the ages, lessons that are new. *Stat magni nominis umbra:* they feel, when they meet us, that though they may have heard the last of Albert the Good, they have not heard the last of Albert the Great. A hundred years back they hoped to dispose of the Church by disposing of the Bible; now their tactics have grown more subtle. They hope to dispose of the Church by disposing of Aristotle. It has become the fashion to gird at us because our whole thought is built up round a philosophical system which was fifteen hundred years old when we assimilated it, and has now ceased to hold the speculative allegiance of mankind. Only the other day I read a book by a popularizer of science, well known in the broadcasting world, whose whole thesis was that Einstein has shewn up Euclid, and if we are not going to believe in Euclid it would be absurd to believe in Aristotle, and if we no longer believe in Aristotle, then Christianity has ceased to count.

It is with happy omen, then, if we may dare to criticize the solemn actions of the Church in terms of human congruity, that the Holy Father has just raised St. Albert to the altars of the Church, and numbered him among her doctors. Not in the sense that the Church is concerned to applaud the physical speculations of the great philosopher, or to regard them as final, when St. Albert himself was not content to regard them as final. Nor even in the sense that Aristotle's metaphysics are the only possible framework of thought in which the Christian world-idea can be stated. Rather because, in the speculative confusion of our time, when men talk as if the theories advanced by natural science were inconsistent with the doctrines of our faith, it is good to look back on a time when Aristotle himself seemed to be an anti-Christian writer, and the attempt to rehabilitate him was regarded with deep suspicion by the old-fashioned. Rather because, when the cry is all for novelty, for further discoveries which shall sweep us away, more and more, from our intellectual bearings, it is well to be reminded that sooner or later human thought always turns back on itself; and the system which was once discredited creeps back into favour again. The modern world lives on its intellectual capital, exploits the prevalent doctrine of the moment in the interest of its heresies; floodlights the universe with a gleam of partial illumination, or darkens the skies with doubt; the Church, who is wiser and older, stores new things and old alike in her treasure-house, and brings them out in their due relation to enrich, permanently, the experience of mankind.

May we go further, and admire the Providence which has left it for a Pope, pre-eminently a man of thought as well as a man of action, to canonize a Saint who was pre-eminently a man of action as well as a man of thought? For, after all, the really surprising thing about St. Albert is not so much the enormous range of learning which won him his title of the Universal Doctor, as the fact that the life which included so much reading and writing, in days when reading and writing were difficult, included also a vast amount of administrative activity; he was not a mere lecturer or regent of studies; he was Provincial of his order in Germany, and for three years a bishop. Well might a contemporary describe him as 'the astonishment and miracle of our times.' How did he manage it all? The secret is out at last; he was a Saint. The tradition of him preserved in his own order and in his own country has been ratified by the solemn judgement of the Church. Too long we have thought of him as merely reflecting the rays of St. Thomas' beatitude; we know now that those who were so intimately associated in their lives, and not divided in their loyalty by death, were not divided, save by a few years, in their entry into a blessed eternity. Master and pupil, they could share with our Blessed Lord and our Blessed Lady the joys of an everlasting reunion.

May St. Albert's prayers bring peace to a distracted Europe; may they enlighten, as he himself enlightened in his time, the darkness of human thought. And may your own order, Reverend Fathers, be worthy of its saintly heritage, and prove ever fertile of scribes instructed in the kingdom of heaven, to bring out of your treasure-house new things and old.

IX

Roger Bacon

*(Preached at his memorial tablet, on the
site of the old Franciscan Friary at Oxford)*

There shall be no remembrance of the wise, no more than
of the fool, for ever; and the times to come shall cover all
things together with oblivion. The learned dieth in like
manner as the unlearned (Eccl 2:16).

R OGER BACON, whose memory is perpetuated by that
tablet in the wall in front of you, is one of the world's
great men. He left behind him a living tradition, in Oxford especially; so that men looked back to him as if he
had been a great magician, something like Doctor Faustus;
and you may still see prints of the gate-house that used to
stand on Folly Bridge, which is described, in the legend
underneath the picture, as Friar Bacon's study. But while
his memory in men's mouths thus passed into something
legendary, his works remained scattered through the libraries of Europe; probably there are more of them to be
unearthed yet. And as these were found and published
he acquired a new reputation in the learned world, as if
he had been a man vastly ahead of his time, both in the
methods of his research and the results of it. Not because
of his most characteristic views, the views he expressed
with most warmth and courage; as, for example, that the
philosophers of his day were all taking the wrong course

75

because they could not study the works of older philosophers in the original Greek and Arabic; or that theology was at fault because it was not strictly based on a careful examination of Holy Scripture, which was, to Roger Bacon, the ultimate source of all knowledge whatsoever. No, the moderns have been interested in Bacon because he did know something about optics, could tell you how to make a telescope or a microscope, though it does not appear that he had either; dreamed, perhaps, of steam traction and of aviation, had a secret recipe for making gunpowder; sought, even, in the very latest fashion, to set out all physical reality in mathematical formulæ. One of the world's great men; we do well to put up a tablet to him.

At the same time, Roger Bacon is not a Saint. He is not, that is to say, a Saint canonized by the Church; we can never say with certainty that this man or that, who has died, is not reigning already in heaven; only God knows that, who can read our consciences. But the character of Bacon, as you find it in his own writings or in the impressions of his contemporaries, is not apt to strike the reader as a saintly character. Indeed, if the truth must be told, within earshot, almost, of all these venerable institutions, Bacon was not much of a Saint—he was more of a don. He had the don's unalterable conviction that all the other dons were going the wrong way about things; that they were not profound enough, not accurate enough; that nothing could be done until the whole of learning had been reorganized on his own lines. It was not that Bacon was attempting to glorify his own order by belittling the work of other orders; he was quite as fierce about Alexan-

der of Hales, the Franciscan, as about anybody else. And
if he lived a troubled life, and incurred the suspicion of
his superiors, it is difficult not to believe that it was partly
his own fault. He had the irritable temperament of the
scholar, and he minced no words when he wanted to put
other people right.

But although he may not have been a Saint, Bacon was
a perfectly good Catholic. He was, in every way, a child
of his age. It is very tempting, but it is a great mistake to
hail him as the prophet born out of due time, who an-
ticipated this or that later movement, and deserves to be
regarded as the father of it. He wanted to revive the study
of Greek, but he is not the forerunner of humanism; he
cared nothing for the classical culture, he only wanted
people to read Aristotle, and the New Testament, in the
original. He believed in getting back to Scripture, but
he was not the forerunner of the Reformation. On the
contrary, he was befriended by a Pope, and everywhere
treats the papacy with due respect; nor is his complaint
against the worldliness of Bishops or prelates, but against
the ignorance of scholars. He shews a wonderful *flair* for
science when you consider the limited possibilities that
existed in his day for the study of it; but he is not the
forerunner of the Empiricists; has no kinship with his
namesake, Francis. To him, as to all the men of his day,
metaphysics was the highest form of science in the human scale; and metaphysics was only the handmaid of
theology. If Roger Bacon came back to Oxford to-day I
believe you would find him quarrelling with all the other
learned men as heartily as ever. The philosophers would
find him a back number and the scholars would find him

a pedant, and the scientists would find him a chopper of logic, and the theologians would find him a fundamentalist; and there would be fresh trouble all round.

But Roger Bacon is dead. And by that I do not mean merely that his soul long since underwent separation from his body, as all souls must. I mean that his very memory is by now a thing of the past, belongs to an old world, which is still the subject of antiquarian interest, but is not near enough to us to feel as if it were a part of ourselves. With the Saints, you see, it is otherwise; just as their bodies, in many cases, have been found uncorrupt long years after they were buried, so their lives remain embalmed for us in the odour of sanctity, belong to us, if we are faithful Catholics, as if they were men of yesterday. Saint Francis is not dead, in the sense in which I am now using the word. He is removed from our company, because he is in heaven; but his story is of yesterday; he is like an elder brother who died, more is the pity, before we were born. You cannot think of him as remote, uncongenial, shut off from us; his sanctity bridges the centuries that lie between us. But Roger Bacon belongs to the past, for all those precocious speculations of his which made him seem ahead of his time. There shall be no remembrance of the wise, no more than of the fool, for ever; and the times to come shall cover all things together with oblivion. The learned dieth in like manner as the unlearned. That is the law under which Roger Bacon is forgotten.

And yet, is he forgotten? Not altogether; not in Oxford. He is remembered here because his own Grey Friars have come back here and will not allow the site of their old residence to be altogether obliterated. So they have chosen Brother Roger as the type, the representative, of all those many Franciscan friars who must be waiting, not far from this spot, for their Resurrection. We are to pray, not 'grant him,' but 'grant them' eternal rest; not only Brother Roger, but all those cloister-mates of his whose names we do not know; the ones who worked for him without acknowledgment, copied out manuscripts for him and verified facts for him and pointed out slips he had made, helped in one way and another to make his name the great name it is; the ones who did not quite approve of him, and thought his studies were all waste of time, if not worse; the ones who laughed at him, and thought him a crack-brained old fellow; the learned people (for there were plenty of others in that beautiful dawn of Oxford scholarship) who never managed to achieve fame like his, and the simple people who were content to be simple people like St. Francis—all the old Grey Friars you must have seen once, walking up and down behind the old battlements, as you came upon Oxford from the south, across the windings of the Thames.

All alike, Brother Roger with the rest of them, belong to the past now; the conditions under which they lived, the problems they had to face, were not our conditions or our problems, and we cannot really put ourselves in their place, or them in ours. The world is so full of anxiety about the present, of speculation about the future, that it has no time to waste, no tears to shed, over the ruined glories of the past. But we, Catholics of Oxford, assemble once a year to remember these fellow-townsmen, fellow-gownsmen of ours, and to pray for their souls; that gracious bond of unity is not destroyed for us by any lapse of years or any change of manners. Let us commend, then, to the mercy of God and to the prayers of his Blessed Mother that restless soul, so long ago laid to rest, and the souls of all who in times past ministered or worshipped in this place; and let us pray also, in this place, for a restoration to the university of the faith in which it was cradled, and of the sacramental life which it once lived by, and has lost.

X

St. Joan of Arc

(Preached to schoolboys at St. Edmund's, Ware)

All these died according to faith, not having received the promises, but beholding them afar off and saluting them, and confessing that they are pilgrims and strangers on the earth. . . . Who by faith conquered kingdoms, wrought justice, obtained promises, stopped the mouths of lions, quenched the violence of fire, escaped the edge of the sword, recovered strength from weakness, became valiant in battle, put to flight the armies of foreigners (Heb 11:13, 33, 34).

I DO NOT know how it is with you, but, for me, almost ever since I can remember hearing it read, this chapter of the Hebrews has exercised a special fascination, has enabled me to follow the story of the Old Testament in a new attitude and with a new interest. The patriarchs as you knew them when you were quite small, whether from picture-books or from the confirmatory evidence supplied by stained-glass windows, were old gentlemen with beards who had their clothes, mostly in rather dowdy purples and browns, hitched up round them in an inconvenient sort of way, and always carried a large stick in one hand and a thurible in the other when, apparently, they were just going out for a walk. Heavy, lifeless figures they seemed, against a flat, conventional background of

81

palm-trees, and you felt it was impossible that they should ever mean anything to you or carry any living message. And then came this chapter of the Hebrews and filled the whole scene with life, set the cardboard palm-trees waving and the long skirts rustling, and everything was astir. It was not simply that they went to the same tailor, they had something in common; there was a secret behind their dignified silence. They died according to faith, not having received the promises, but beholding them afar off and saluting them; God providing some better thing for us, that without us they should not be perfected.

By faith he—that is, Abraham—abode in the land, dwelling in tents with Isaac and Jacob, the co-heirs of the same promise; for he looked for a city that hath foundations, whose builder and maker is God. He managed to live in tents, to endure that uncomfortable, makeshift, draughty sort of existence—how? Because he looked for a city that hath foundations, whose builder and maker is God. That is the faith of the Old Testament Saints, to live as strangers in a transitory world on the strength of a promise—a promise they knew they would not live to see fulfilled. Faith is the substance of things hoped for, the evidence of things that appear not. And you will find that same common quality among the Saints of the Christian dispensation. They lived in very different ages and very different countries; their circumstances differed widely, and their manner of life. Yesterday we had the office of St. John Baptist de la Salle, who rose to sanctity in the exercise of a very humble and a very humdrum occupation, and one that does not often produce Saints: he was a schoolmaster. And to-day the infallible Voice of Christendom is raising to the altars of the Church, as she was long since raised to the glories of heaven, the heroine of a very different career: a village girl who really did conquer kingdoms, really did recover strength from weakness, became valiant in battle, put to flight the armies of foreigners—yes, St. Joan of Arc. How nice it sounds, 'St. Joan of Arc.' But through all the history of sanctity you will find this same quality persisting—the quality of realizing that what we see and touch and feel are transitory things and unreal, and that the solid things, the substantial things, are the things that appear not, the world we only grasp by faith.

And I am insisting on that particular quality this morning because I think it is one that stands out with quite extraordinary clearness in St. Joan's life: she did really live for a promise, and we know that the promise came true, but she did not—not in this life. She was very young, you know. Did you realize that she was less than twenty years old when she was burnt at the stake? It is not true that she dressed as a man; she dressed as a boy. When she was only thirteen years old, at the age when the other boys and girls were fidgeting and playing the fool during Mass, as people did in those days, she could hardly go out of doors without hearing the voices of Saints and Angels talking to her. And those voices dominated her life; they echoed so loudly in her ears that all the world's noises were drowned for her. People said: 'It is very silly of a small girl like you to think she can go and see the King' —she did not hear them. And the King, as you know, disguised himself and hid among his courtiers, and she went straight up to him: 'But I am not the King,' he said, 'that is the King over there.' 'Oh, yes, you are; I have come to raise the siege of Orleans and crown you king at Rheims.' It was no good; the voices had told her about it. And I suppose when she had been appointed Chief of the Army the General Staff would always be raising military difficulties about re-entrant angles and being enfiladed by arquebus-fire, and so on, but it did not make a bit of difference to her, she always did what the voices told her— they were close to her ear, you see, and the criticisms of the General Staff were only a distant echo. She went out, not knowing whither she went.

And of course she had disappointments. After the first few victories, after the crowning of the King, the people she had come to save contented themselves with a partial conquest, and hung about making treaties and de-mobilizing troops. And truly, if she had been mindful of that from whence she came out, she had doubtless time to return; she could have gone back to Domrémy and rested on her laurels. But the ingratitude and apathy of the court affected her no more than its honours had done; she simply went on obeying the voices. And the French lords played her false, and she was taken prisoner. But she endured, as seeing him who is invisible.

And then came the hardest time of all. I do not think she minded being in prison; I do not think she minded the threat of execution; that was not why she tried to escape. No, it was simply that it seemed quite obvious to her she was to deliver France—the voices had told her so —and France was not yet delivered. And so she went to the stake, her hopes still unfulfilled, but never doubting for an instant that the voices were true. Five years later the King entered Paris; twenty-two years later, England had no possessions left on French soil. She believed that he was faithful who had promised, not having received the promises, but beholding them afar off and saluting them. She could not foresee that her unjust condemnation would be reversed, point by point, twenty-five years after her death: she could not foresee that, nearly five hundred years after her death, France, once more liberated, would receive the tidings of her canonization by the tribunal to which, in life, she never ceased to appeal, the tribunal of the Holy See. But she believed that he was faithful who had promised.

That, then, is her great witness, as it is the witness of all the Saints: that is her capital contribution to our Christian hope—we know, because the Saints have told us so, that it is the things of this world that are shams and shadows, and the real things and the solid things are the things we cannot see. Our Saviour Christ has ascended up into heaven, and a cloud received him from our sight, but we are not therefore to think of the spiritual world as something far removed from us, only to be reached by a supreme effort of thought. On the contrary, the spiritual world is all about us: the voices are still there, only St. Joan could hear them and we cannot. I wonder whose fault that is? Blessed are the pure in heart, for they shall see God.

> The Angels keep their ancient places;
>   Turn but a stone, and start a wing:
> 'Tis ye, 'tis your estranged faces
>   That miss the many-splendoured thing.

> But, when so sad thou canst not sadder,
>   Cry, and upon thy so sore loss
> Shall shine the traffic of Jacob's ladder
>   Pitched between Heaven and Charing Cross.

This is no other but the house of God, and the gate of Heaven. When we keep, as to-day, the festival of the Dedication of a Church, this earthly edifice is a sort of sacrament to us, a type of the true city which hath foundations, whose builder and maker is God: of the temple that is built in a world beyond the reach of our sense, by a heavenly Architect, the blows of whose mallet, the polishing strokes of whose chisel, we call pain in this world, and defeat, and loss. Whither may God of his great mercy bring us, that we may see with open vision, among the choir of Virgins that are our Lady's handmaids, the Saint whose glorious merits the Church commemorates to-day.

XI

King Henry the Sixth

(*Preached at St. Catharine's, Chipping Campden*)

These are they whom we had some time in derision, and for a parable of reproach. We fools esteemed their life madness, and their end without honour. Behold, how they are numbered among the children of God, and their lot is among the saints (Wis 5:3⁻5).

FOUR HUNDRED and fifty-five years since, a week ago last Saturday, died the only king of England since the Conquest who has ever been within measurable distance of being raised to the altars of the Church. And because, in our day, there is some hope that his cause will be proceeded with afresh after a long lapse of centuries; because I am particularly bound to him as the Founder of the school at which I was educated, I want to represent to you very briefly this morning the true facts about King Henry the Sixth, and to ask—if what you hear interests you—your prayers for his eventual beatification.

King Henry the Sixth? The mind fumbles nervously in the dusty pigeon-holes of memory. Echoes from the small green Gardiner respond unwillingly to the call. Yes, Henry the Sixth, let me see, was not he the king who was always going mad? An innocent creature, to be sure, not responsible for all the calamities which befell England during his reign; his murder in prison was, I quite agree, one of the most brutal in English history. But . . . a Saint? Surely this harmless type of character, under-developed and barely capable for better or worse of moral action, has nothing to do with the manly virtues of the Saints? They felt temptation, and triumphed over it; they dominated their fellow-men, left their mark on the world through sheer force of character. Surely you are not going to set up this weakling, this half-idiot, beside men like Dunstan, and Anselm, and Thomas More?

These are they whom we had in derision, and for a parable of reproach. We fools esteemed their life madness, and their end without honour. Behold, how they are numbered among the children of God, and their lot is among the Saints. . . . Let me tell you a story. Possibly it is not true, but it is a story which was affirmed on oath and duly chronicled at the time. A little while after King Henry the Sixth died, when it had begun to be rumoured that miracles were being wrought through his prayers, a near neighbour of yours, a certain John Robins of Inkberrow, was making his way to Stratford-on-Avon. And it will have been soon after Abbot's Moreton, where he turned into the main road, that he met with another countryman, George Luffar, from Crowle, who began to talk to him about the holy King Henry and his wonderful miracles. I daresay George Luffar was a tiresome enthusiast, but anyhow John Robins got weary of it, said he did not believe a word of it, said that King Henry was just an innocent creature who hardly knew his right hand from his left, and no more a Saint than anyone else. And so they went on arguing until they got to Stratford. The same day, while he was in Stratford, John Robins went stone blind. There was no explanation of it, and there was no cure for it, until he vowed that he would make a pilgrimage to King Henry's tomb at Windsor—a vow which was afterwards duly paid—and then he recovered his sight on the spot.

Well, I would not trouble you with that story if it were the only story of its kind. But it is one out of one hundred and seventy-four similar stories which are preserved for us in a manuscript now kept at the British Museum. And we know, from that manuscript, that in St. George's Chapel at Windsor they kept a list which contained the record of at least three hundred and sixty-eight miraculous cures and deliverances as the result of prayers offered to King Henry; all of which date during the thirty years between his death in 1471 and the end of that century. What does it all mean? It means that at the end of the fifteenth century the pilgrimage to Windsor was one of the great English pilgrimages, like those to St. Thomas at Canterbury and our Lady at Walsingham. It means that in churches all over the country pictures and statues of King Henry were being put up as if he were one of the Saints—a dozen or so of them may still be seen to-day —that lights were kept burning, and hymns were written in his honour. It means that in those days the natural thing to do, if you were in any trouble, was to appeal to a dead king for his prayers. Why, in the reign of Richard the Third, who was King Henry's murderer, there was a girl over at Honeybourne, called Agnes Freeman, who suffered from what was called the King's Evil; it was a skin disease which could be cured, men said, only by the touch of the reigning monarch—and so it continued down to the day when Dr. Johnson was touched for the King's Evil by Queen Anne. But Agnes Freeman did not go to Richard the Third; she went to the dead king's tomb instead, and found relief from her malady there.

Now, it is quite true that King Henry is not the only popular hero who has been regarded as a Saint by the people who could remember him. The body of Simon de Montfort, the leader of the Barons against the king two hundred years earlier, was kept in the Abbey Church at Evesham, and there is record of miracles happening there. But there is this difference, you see; the devotion to Simon de Montfort died out: the devotion to King Henry did not die out, it was simply swamped by the Reformation. In 1528, the year before Thomas Cranmer became Archbishop of Canterbury, it is historically certain that the envoys of King Henry the Eighth at Rome, while they were urging the Pope to sanction the divorce from Catherine of Aragon, were also urging him to proceed with the beatification of King Henry the Sixth. And the Pope was perfectly willing, he was only waiting for the arrival of fresh evidence from England. And that evidence never came, because the breach between England and Rome came first. The cause had dropped, but the devotion to King Henry did not drop. It is historically certain that pilgrims from Devonshire and Cornwall were coming in large numbers all the way to Windsor as late as the year 1543. 1543, that is nearly seventy years after King Henry the Sixth died, and only half a dozen years before the Mass was abolished in England. England did not lose her faith in King Henry until she lost her faith in the Catholic Church.

Well, I have taken the risk of giving you all this dull lecture in history because, as I say, the reopening of the cause at Rome after nearly four hundred years does seem to be practical politics just now. But nothing will come of it unless people in England will offer prayers for that intention. After all, St. Joan of Arc was neglected for more than four hundred years and then canonized; and now that England, more than ever since the Reformation, is beginning to count among the Catholic countries of Europe, it would be a pity if through some want of patriotism, some want of feeling for our Catholic past, we missed the opportunity of publicly invoking a Saint of our own royal lineage. Pray, then, for his beatification, you who love the English countryside which he loved; and commit to him sometimes your prayers for temporal or spiritual favours; if experience goes for anything, it will not be in vain.

We esteemed their life madness. It is true that twice, during the fifty years of his life, King Henry was deprived, for a time, of the use not only of his senses, but apparently of his limbs. The attack, upon either occasion, lasted less than two months. For the rest, although he was a weak king in stormy times, nobody ever doubted that he had the full use of his reason. The founder of Eton, and of King's College, Cambridge—and in either case he drew up the statutes himself, with particular care—has left to the nation a legacy which is more enduring than those of most English monarchs. There was, in his whole character, a child-like innocence which the men of his own day took for sanctity; it was left for later generations to suggest that this innocence was a form of feeblemindedness.

Is it, perhaps, that in our day we have lost the faculty for appreciating sheer innocence, for understanding the temperament of one who is brutally treated by his enemies, yet bears it all without complaint? If so, I think that King Henry has yet a work to do in schooling and in softening our English hearts.

XII

St. Thomas More

Thus did this man die, leaving not only to young men, but also to the whole nation, the memory of his death for an example of virtue and fortitude (2 Mac 6:31).

THE TEXT which I have just read to you refers to Eleazar, one of the scribes, who suffered martyrdom under King Antiochus for the traditions of the Jewish religion. As a sign of apostasy from that religion, he, like many others, was bidden to eat swine's flesh, which (as you know) was forbidden under the ancient law. Kindly officials offered him, instead, a piece of some other meat which was clean according to the law of Moses; so that he could avoid the defilement as long as he would allow it to be thought that he had conformed with Antiochus' edict. His answer was a noble one; he would rather suffer martyrdom than give scandal to the younger men of his race by pretending to break the law in his old age. He died, it seems, under scourging.

You will not be at a loss to understand why I am recalling to you, this evening, the memory of unhappy things that took place long ago. The history conveys a striking parallel to other unhappy things which happened not so very long ago, only four hundred years ago yesterday. On July 6, 1535, a great Englishman died who has just been raised to the altars of the Church as St. Thomas More.

93

He died, like Eleazar, for something which seemed to many people of his time almost a scruple, almost a technical point; refusing to take an oath in support of a new statute, because there was something in the preamble to the statute of which your conscience disapproved! Oh, you may be sure that St. Thomas More had no lack of plausible excuses if he had wanted to avoid the crown of martyrdom; no lack of sincere people who urged him to take refuge in them. Never, I suppose, was man so tempted both by friends and foes to abandon his purpose. His own wife, his own daughter took the part of his enemies, and entered into a loving conspiracy to save him from himself. But to friend and foe alike he opposed the impenetrable wall of his good-natured banter.

You see, he realized, long before other men of his time, that what stood before England was a complete parting of the ways. He saw that, in the conditions of his time, you must needs throw in your lot either with the old faith or with the heresies that were beginning to spring up all over Europe; that a nation which defied the authority of the Pope, although it might do so merely in the name of national independence, would be forced, sooner or later, into the camp of the heretic. It is amazing to us, looking back upon all the intervening centuries have brought, that so many good men of that age—men who were afterwards confessors for the faith—were hoodwinked for the moment into following the King when he incurred the guilt of schism. But perhaps if we could think ourselves back rather more successfully into the conditions of the time, we should pardon them the more readily; and for that reason we should feel even greater admiration for the few men who, like our martyr, were wise enough to see what was happening. It was a time of national crisis, a time of intellectual ferment. There were only a few people who kept their heads, and those few who kept their heads lost their heads, like St. Thomas More.

Much, naturally, has been said, much has been written in the past few months about him and about the holy Bishop of Rochester who preceded him to his death. His portrait has become familiar to us afresh; his praises are sounded everywhere, even in the most unlikely quarters. What I should like to draw your attention to, this evening, is a single fact about the life and fame of a many-sided man. This fact—that his canonization has been a bewilderment and a blow to the moderns, precisely because he was himself one of the moderns. He belongs to the new world which came to its birth at the Renaissance; of that new world he is a prophet and a pioneer. And, being all that, he gave his life, unquestioningly and unquestionably, for something which our moderns look upon as belonging wholly to that older world which is dead—I mean, the Holy Catholic Church.

It is a curious thing about the attitude of our non-Catholic friends towards the Catholic Saints; they always contrive to discredit, in one of two ways, their witness to the faith. Either they will say: 'This was a very unpleasant, narrow-minded man, of ridiculous personal habits; and if that is what Saints are like we would sooner hear no more of them,' or they will say: 'Yes, this man was indeed a Saint; but then he was not really a Roman Catholic. He was just a good Christian, as I and my wife are; he only happened to be in communion with the Pope because everybody was in those days.' They divide our calendar, in fact, into the nice Saints who do credit to Christianity rather than to the Church, and the nasty Saints who do no credit to anybody. St. Francis, they will say; yes, what a charming character; what meekness, what cheerfulness, what love of animals! But then, St. Francis was not a bit like a Roman Catholic. On the other hand, a man like St. Thomas à Becket, although they admit that his martyrdom was an unfortunate incident, they dismiss altogether from consideration because his particular qualities, his salient qualities anyhow, were not the particular qualities which they happen to admire. And the Church gets no credit either way.

It is being a great puzzle to these people what to make of St. Thomas More. So long as he was simply Thomas More it was all right; they were prepared to admire him as a pioneer of modern thought, or to praise him as a man who gave his life for his convictions, however mistaken. But now, we have taken to calling him a Saint, and it is difficult to see which of the two categories he is to fit into. Is he to be regarded as one of the Saints who were not really nice men, were not really admirable men? But nobody can help loving Thomas More; nobody can help admiring Thomas More. Or are they going to regard him as one of the Saints who were not really Roman Catholics? But unfortunately, his death makes that impossible. In life, if you will, he can be regarded as one of the moderns, as a pioneer of the Renaissance, as a cultured, liberal, broad-minded man, all that they are prepared to admire. But in his death, look at it what way you will, he is plainly a Catholic. He exploded the mine of controversy twenty-five years before its time; forced an issue between England and the Holy See before England had ever realized that it was going Protestant. Is it possible that we are to have, after all, an indisputably Catholic Saint whom, nevertheless, our non-Catholic neighbours will find themselves compelled to admire?

Let us pause for a little over that apparent contrast in the life of a man whose sympathies clearly belonged to the new order of things, who yet died as a protest on behalf of the old order of things. Let me explain to you, at the risk of seeming to give you a lecture in history, what I mean when I say that St. Thomas More has to take rank among the moderns. Of course, there is a certain sense in which all the English martyrs belong to our modern world, as compared with the English Saints who went before them. If you think of St. Edmund of Canterbury, or St. Richard of Chichester, the last English Saints who lived before Reformation times, you inevitably think of them, if I may say so without irreverence, as people in stained-glass windows, belonging to an era altogether different from our own. We do not know what they looked like, because there was little art of portraiture in their day, and of the art there was few specimens are preserved to us. And the medieval world to which they belonged is something we read about in history books, but something which has, so it appears, no living contact with our own. But our martyrs, even under Henry the Eighth and Queen Elizabeth, are living, human figures; in many cases we have authentic portraits, their writings have come down to us in abundance—we can imagine, or so we think, what it was like to live under the Tudors. Yes, the English martyrs are nearer to us than the Saints who went before them; but in the case of St. Thomas More it goes deeper than that. He was a humanist, one of the most prominent figures in that revival of learning, that broadening of culture, which followed upon what we call the Renaissance. All that, you say, is very vague; I am using long words, which leave no particular impression on your mind. Very well, then, let me try to put it in the concrete a little, and consider how it was that the men of the Renaissance differed from the men of the Middle Ages.

First, the men of the Renaissance looked backwards at history more than their predecessors did. The old classical authors of Greece and Rome, long hidden away in the shelves of dusty libraries, came to light and were studied eagerly. They tried to feel and to understand what other men thought, long centuries ago before our Lord came. And St. Thomas More was steeped in all that; although he was such a busy man of affairs, he was one of the scholars of his age, the intimate friend of the great Dutchman, Erasmus. Many historians will tell you that the Renaissance, by opening men's minds to new avenues of learning, paved the way for the Reformation. It may be so, but among the greatest leaders of the Renaissance you will find St. Thomas More, who died a martyr for the Catholic faith.

In the second place, the men of the Renaissance looked outwards at a world that had grown larger than the world which their fathers knew. 'The world,' as it was known to the Middle Ages, meant—what? Europe, and the north coast of Africa, and a few strange, half-fabulous countries in the East, which only a few unreliable travellers had vis-

ited. By the year 1500 Columbus had discovered America, Cabot had sailed to Canada, and Vasco da Gama had
doubled the Cape of Good Hope. Within a quarter of a
century the known world had suddenly grown to three or
four times its old size. Men's minds were fascinated by the
thought that there were strange races in distant parts of
the earth whose customs and traditions and way of looking at life were wholly different from their own. And not
least, the mind of St. Thomas More. Every schoolboy
knows that he wrote a book called *Utopia*, describing the
habits of an imaginary people on some remote island, and
using that means to satirize the shortcomings of his own
day. That imaginary island owed its existence, you may
say, to the discoveries of explorers among real islands,
twenty or thirty years before the book was written. The
mind of such a man, clearly, was not bounded as men's
minds were bounded in the Middle Ages by the horizon
of Christendom. And yet it was for Christendom that St.
Thomas More died on the scaffold.

In the third place—this is more difficult to explain—
the men of the Renaissance looked inwards, turned back
upon themselves, watched their own thoughts, instead of
being entirely wrapped up in objects outside themselves
which challenged their attention. The proper study of
mankind, said a great poet, is Man; and the men of the
Renaissance are called Humanists because they rediscov-
ered, in a way, the greatness and the complexity and the
absorbing interest of Man. You will find that all through
the sixteenth century; you will find it in the art of Shake-
speare, you will find it among the theologians of that age,
in the enormously increased study of moral theology. And

you will find it in the character of a man like St. Thomas More; exemplified especially in that gift of self-criticism and of irony which distinguishes him; what we call nowadays, roughly, the sense of humour. A man passionately interested in men, allowing for their temperaments and sympathizing with their weaknesses. Yet a Humanist, we see, could also be a man of stern principle; it was because he would not condone the weaknesses of the king who had been his friend that St. Thomas More died.

All that enlargement of outlook, backwards, outwards, inwards, makes St. Thomas More one of the moderns. If he lived in our own day—let us put it crudely—you can imagine him arguing over Plato with Dean Inge, or constructing imaginary worlds in collaboration with Mr. H. G. Wells, or answering jest with jest, irony with irony, in a conversation with Mr. Bernard Shaw. And if he had died in his bed, before the attack on the monasteries, before the question of King Henry's divorce ever arose, just imagine what the world would be saying of him. They would be telling us that he was, of course, a Roman Catholic, because that was how he had been brought up—indeed, in his youth he had been through a period of fanaticism, in which he thought of joining the Carthusians. But his whole mind, they would be telling us, had completely outgrown the narrow horizons of his youth; he was a critic of abuses in the Church, he was a friend of those Continental scholars who made, in great part, the Reformation. And had he lived, they would be telling us, this patron of the new learning would certainly have thrown in his lot with the Reformers, with Cranmer and Cromwell; perhaps, as an old man, he would have helped to build up the sonorous language of the Anglican prayer-book. All that they would be saying, were it not for the unfortunate fact that he died a Roman Catholic, died because he was a Roman Catholic, died because he saw that you could not be a Catholic without being a Roman.

That seems to me the really extraordinary quality about our new Saint, that he could bring forth out of his treasure, like the householder of Our Lord's parable, things new and old; that he belonged to the new world, and yet died for something against which the new world was shortly to revolt. If he had been some member of the old English aristocracy, suspicious of the Tudors because they were upstarts, and resentful against their efforts to consolidate the power of the Crown as against the nobility—then we might have been afraid that political considerations affected his attitude. But it was not so; he was one of the new men, one of the King's friends, the last man in the world to stand upon ancient privilege for its own sake. If he had been some pedantic follower of a philosophy which had gone out of fashion, resolutely set against all new-fangled ideas, then we might have been afraid that there was something of mere human obstinacy, mere pig-headedness, that entered into his protest. But it was not so; as we have seen, he was a pillar and a patron of the new learning. If he had been some bluff, rude country squire, always ready to pick a quarrel with his neighbours for the sheer love of a fight, careless of what suffering he underwent himself or inflicted on others, then we might have been afraid that he took the risks he took, faced the scaffold as he did, out of a kind of insensibility, valuing his life little because he had never acquired the art of enjoying life intelligently. But no, St. Thomas More was a sensitive man, of our modern type, very reluctant, as we know, to inflict punishment on others, and fully alive to the horrors of his own situation, as you or I would be. It was not temperament, it was not perversity, but sheer love of the faith he had been bred in that made a martyr of St. Thomas More.

I wonder whether there is not something Providential, I mean something that we can recognize as specially Providential, about the delays which have attended the canonization of St. Thomas More and St. John Fisher, humanly speaking so long overdue? Whether, I mean, God does not mean us to understand that these two, and St. Thomas More especially, are fitting patrons for our own age, because our own age is in so many ways like theirs? For in our age—it is a commonplace to say it—a new humanism flourishes, something like the humanism of four hundred years ago, but for better or worse a great advance upon it. We have dug further back than ever St. Thomas More and his contemporaries did into the history of our race; unearthed the relics of civilizations far older than those of Greece or Rome, pushed back, by tens of thousands of years, the limits of human history. We have not discovered fresh continents—there were none to discover; but we have entered into closer contact with men of alien ideas, studied their history, and puzzled out the secret of their attitude towards life. And we have turned back more than ever on ourselves; analysed the background of our own minds, tried to trace the origins of our own mental processes. Our age, more than ever, is lost in admiration of man's greatness, so as to forget the God who made us;

at the same time, more tender towards man's weaknesses, more tolerant of his wrong-doing, more merciful to his faults. And in this age of increased reverence for man you and I have got to live, reminding ourselves and reminding our neighbours of that higher reverence which is due to God.

Times like these, do not let us deceive ourselves about it, are difficult to live in for a Catholic who loves his faith. There is a continual apparent contrast between the restless speculations of the modern intellect, and those abiding certainties by which we live. The question continually arises: Is such and such a view, which I see propounded in the newspapers, consistent with Catholic truth? Is such and such a political expedient, which I see prominent men are advocating, justifiable in the light of Catholic doctrine? We are hurried along breathlessly by the spirit of the age in which we live, yet protesting all the time, questioning all the time. Our neighbours, our non-Catholic neighbours, look upon us as an obscure survival from the Middle Ages, a kind of museum piece, whose beliefs they find it interesting to study, but impossible to share. Here and there, one or two of our Catholic friends drop out of the ranks, abandon their religion for no better reason than that they have been caught by the glamour of modern movements. There is no acute conflict, but we are perpetually ill at ease, like a ship that drags its anchor.

In such times, let us thank God's mercy for giving us the example and the protection of a great Saint, our own fellow-countryman, who knew how to absorb all that was best in the restless culture of his day, yet knew at once, when the time came, that he must make a stand here;

that he must give no quarter to the modern world here. His remembrance has long been secure in the praise of posterity; it only remained for us to be assured by the infallible voice of the Church, what we could not doubt already, that he is with our Blessed Lady and the Saints in heaven. He knows our modern needs, let us turn to him in our modern troubles; his prayers will not be lacking for the great country he loved so, for the great city in which he lived and died.

XIII

St. Ignatius Loyola

Then his son Judas, called Machabeus, rose up in his stead; and all his brethren helped him, and all they that had joined themselves to his father, and they fought with cheerfulness the battle of Israel (1 Mac 3:1).

THERE ARE few stories, I suppose, in history, so epical as that of the resistance made by Juda under the Machabees to the power of Syrian tyrants; there have been few movements which combined, so perfectly as theirs did, the twin aspirations of religion and patriotism. That the Church holds them in special honour is witnessed by the curious fact that they, almost alone among all the heroes of the Old Testament, have a feast and a Mass and an Office dedicated yearly to their honour. We Catholics are not always very well read in the Old Testament; let me just remind you briefly, then, of what it was these men did, and what was the quarrel in which they fought.

The conquests of Alexander the Great at the end of the third century before Christ had let loose all over the East, as far as the borders of India, a flood of Greek influence and rather superficial Greek civilization. At his death, his chief captains, like the marshals of Napoleon, ascended royal thrones; in Egypt, the Ptolemies, in Syria, the Seleuci. When war arose between these two dynasties, as it did a generation later, it was inevitable that the little people of Juda, with their territory lying on the high road from Syria to Egypt, should be swept into the current of world politics once more. And that meant grave peril to their national faith, and to their mission as the one people in the world which maintained, in its integrity, the worship of the one true God. Gentile influences began to creep in—the Greek tolerance of false worship and of superstition, the Greek cult of beauty, the Greek contempt for morals. There was a party in Judaea itself favourable to this foreign culture. And when Antiochus Epiphanes came up with an army to Jerusalem, and sacked it, and robbed the temple treasures, and set up heathen worship in the Holy Places, it was not the whole nation that protested and suffered. Some Jews, in that degenerate age, were ready to conform to the new order of things; they consented to eat the flesh of swine, forbidden to them by the Mosaic law, in witness of their apostasy. But there was a remnant which remained faithful; and it was these who, under the leadership of the Machabean brethren, won back the holy city, and defeated army after army sent against them by their oppressors, and re-established the independence of their country until it was finally lost through the conquests of the Romans a century later.

I would like you to notice three points especially about the triumphant career of these patriots. The first is this —that we are dealing with a succession of men, all of the same family, who all shewed the same spirit and maintained the same policy with equal fearlessness. You do not often find that in history; you find it very seldom in the history of the Jews. Now and again, by the special decrees of Providence, some great prophet appoints, before his death, another great prophet to succeed him; so Moses appoints Josue, and Elias appoints Eliseus. But as a rule the great figures of Old Testament history are solitary figures, and when they disappear there is nobody, or worse than nobody, to succeed them. The sons of Gedeon, one of the greatest of the Judges, the sons of the high priest Eli, the sons of the prophet Samuel, how soon they degenerated, and disgraced the traditions of their family! But Mathathias, dying at the very outset of the campaign, leaves five sons. Of these, Eleazar is killed in the first important battle, but Judas is left in command; only for a year or two, then he is killed in battle, and his brother John treacherously slain. Jonathan succeeds, and for eight years keeps the enemies of religion at bay. At last he is caught in an ambush; but there is still one left; Simon, the last of the brothers, eclipses the triumphs of his predecessors, and during the eight years of his leadership the nation flourishes as it has never flourished since, I suppose, the time of King Solomon. One patriot with five sons to succeed him, and not a single weak link in the chain; here is a rare accident of history.

And the next point is this, that before they could muster their forces, and dispute with the heathen the mastery of their native soil, it was necessary for them to take refuge in the hill country, in their native city of Modin. Mathathias cried with a loud voice, 'Everyone that hath zeal for the law and maintaineth the testament, let him follow me,' and he and his sons fled into the mountains, and left all that they had in the city. It was in those same mountains that David had taken refuge, when he fled from the persecution of King Saul; and he has sung of those outlaw strongholds of his in words that still echo through the sanctuaries of Christendom; 'I will lift up mine eyes to the hills, whence cometh my help,' 'the Lord hath brought me out, and set me up upon a rock of stone'—the Machabees took him for their model, and retired to the hill fastnesses till they had gathered the strength needed for their effort.

And the third point is this; that the Machabees did resolve to defeat the heathen with their own weapons. There was always a party among the Jews, at any moment of national crisis, which was for a non-resistance policy, what they called 'waiting on the Lord'; if God saw fit to deliver them, he would do so by a miracle; no need, then, to oppose force with force. There were such men in the time of the Machabees; and in particular there was a party of refugees which refused to fight on the Sabbath day, and was exterminated by massacre rather than break the letter of the Mosaic law by fighting on the day of rest. And we are told that the Machabees took, in view of that incident, a remarkable decision. 'Whosoever shall come against us to fight on the Sabbath day, we will fight against him, and we will not all die, as our brethren that were slain in the secret places.' If they were to do battle for the law of Moses, they must not press the letter of that law so as to imperil the whole success of their enterprise.

It is difficult for any English Catholic to read the two books of Machabees without being reminded of the situation in Europe four hundred years ago. It was, after all, the Renaissance, the rediscovery of the classical authors, and the return to classical models, which paved the way for the Continental Reformation; it was the scepticism of the Greeks that infected the pure atmosphere of the Middle Ages, as it had infected, long before, the pure atmosphere of Jewish life. And the result, in our own country as in many others, was a profanation of holy places, a breaking down of altars, and carrying away of consecrated things; so that the very words of Scripture seem as if they had been written for our use. 'The Holy Places are come into the hands of strangers, her Temple is become as a man without honour; the vessels of her glory are carried away captive. . . . Our sanctuary and our beauty and our glory is laid waste, and the Gentiles have defiled them.'

As the invasion of Antiochus had the effect of producing a reaction among the Jews, a return to stricter observance of the law and greater jealousy for the honour of the true God, so under the hand of Providence the apostasy of the sixteenth century produced, in Europe, that return to loyalty and that increase of Catholic zeal which we call the Counter-Reformation. And although St. Ignatius, when he founded the Company of Jesus, was not specially concerned to combat the errors of Luther, and turned his eyes rather to the Mohammedan world, at first, his dreams of spiritual conquest, it is clear to us now that his Institute came just in time to put itself at the head of the Counter-Reformation movement, and save Europe for the faith. I hope you will not think me fanciful, then, Reverend Fathers, if I see in the Machabean brethren a type of that little Company of free-lances with which your holy founder defied the forces of his age, and fought with cheerfulness the battle of Israel.

I said that the Machabees, unlike other Jewish patriots,

had the advantage of being a series; their greatness did not die with Mathathias, or with Judas, or with Jonathan. So your Order is distinguished, I think, among the religious orders by the permanence of its tradition and its unfailing output of sanctity. From the year 1491 to the year 1716 there was never a moment at which there was not a Jesuit Saint alive on earth. I mean by Saints only such as have, by now, been canonized by the Church; is there any other order, I wonder, that could make a similar boast? And what you can say of actual sanctity, you can say also of the spirit of the Order. The Society of Jesus has not, like other institutes, its periods of revival and its periods of decay; it retains, beyond precedent, the memory of its first fervour. Where men complain of it, they complain not of its relaxation, but of its activity; it has been suppressed, but it has never been reformed. Let us thank God for that first, this unintermittent spiritual energy which has marked the history of the Society for four hundred years.

I said that the Machabees, as the condition of their successful resistance, had first of all to withdraw into the mountains and rally their forces there. 'He and his sons fled into the mountains, and left all that they had in the city'—it is surely, under Providence, the long and careful novitiate of the Order, with the spirit of detachment it produces, that has kept the spirit of St. Ignatius alive. Other institutes have encouraged retirement from the world, and access to the mountain-life of contemplation, as an end in itself; they have exiled themselves from the corruptions of the world. With the sons of St. Ignatius it is otherwise; they have retired to those mountains that they might swoop down all the more successfully on the world they seemed to have abandoned, and conquer it with the impetus of their descent. Men have talked and written foolishly as if the strength of the Society lay in its guardianship of a secret, a secret oath, or a code of secret instructions, or something of that kind. But it is not so; the path by which it guards its mountain stronghold is not a secret path, but one plain to view, discouraging access only by its steepness and ruggedness; it is called 'The Spiritual Exercises.' The secret of the Order is a secret which it has been giving away, century after century, to anyone who will try its efficacy for himself.

I said that the Machabees determined to meet the world with its own weapons; that they abandoned the policy of non-resistance which some of their partisans would have maintained, would not even be bound, in case of hostile attack, by the prescriptions of the Mosaic law which defined the Sabbath rest. They realized that armies trained under the Macedonian discipline could not be kept at bay by the same methods which had repelled, in time gone by, attack from the barbarians of the desert. And that, surely, is the astounding thing about St. Ignatius, if you view his influence on history merely from its human side. Long ago, when I was a Protestant, I remember playing some after-dinner game in which you were expected to write down the names of the six greatest men—I think it was —in history, and surprising my company by including St. Ignatius' name among the list. When you read the beginning of his story, you are impressed with the feeling that you have here a thoroughly unpractical man; the last, you might say, of the knights-errant. He was saturated him-

self, like Don Quixote, in the adventurous romances of
his period, and he has developed, as a result, a Quixotic
habit of mind. He will pursue and kill the Moor who
has blasphemed our Lady—no, on second thoughts, he
will give his horse its reins and see which path it takes.
He will go out to the Holy Land and convert the Turks;
he will dress oddly to make the street-boys laugh at him
—oh, a generous character, a lovable character, who will
possibly do great things, but will he leave behind him any
permanent legacy to be remembered by? And then, all of
a sudden, you find that this last of the knights-errant has
turned into the first of the great business men. He has
developed, heaven only knows how, capacities for organization which might have enabled him to name his own
salary as the director of any modern enterprise; he can
make the world his chess-board.

He saw—not, surely, by any natural light—that the old
fabric of Christendom was breaking up around him; and
that, in the troublous days which followed, the Church
would need a body of free-lances, not specializing in one
department or following one way of life, but ready to
adapt themselves to any environment, to take up any form
of legitimate activity, to go anywhere and do anything for
the greater glory of God. And all that would need a spirit
of obedience for which the existing religious Orders, with
their carefully defined spheres of activity, were unsuited.
A flying column of picked troops, throwing themselves
into all the multifarious life of the modern world, yet
always with the glory of God before their eyes. All the
world's caricatures of Jesuit aims and Jesuit methods, all
its cant use of the very word Jesuit, are a kind of distorted

compliment. The modern world knows that the Society is a match for it, and takes its revenge in abuse.

I have left myself little time to draw a moral from all this for us others. Let us propose to ourselves a lesson of warning. When the Machabean brethren were at the height of their success, Joseph the son of Zacharias, and Azarias captain of the soldiers, said, 'Let us also get us a name, and let us fight with the Gentiles that are round about us'; they were routed and put to flight, because, says the sacred author, 'they did not hearken to Judas and his brethren, thinking that they should do manfully; but they were not of the seed of those men by whom salvation was brought to Israel.' How easy it is to excuse ourselves for mingling freely in all society and in all pursuits of the world around us, thinking that we will be all the more effective Christians for being thorough men of the world; how easy it is for us to get the worst of that encounter, and lose our standards, and be dragged down to the world's own level, if we are not of the seed of those men by whom salvation is to be brought to the Church! Before we can do any good in the world or to the world, we must go up to the mountains and learn to separate ourselves from the world; for us, as for the sons of St. Ignatius, the preface to any victory must be a retreat. The Saint whom we celebrate to-day bequeathed, not only to his own institute but to Christendom in general, one legacy for which, even if he had left no Order behind him, Christendom would owe him eternal gratitude—the Spiritual Exercises. It is generally so hard to imagine, 'What advice would such and such a Saint give to me, if I could meet him nowadays in the flesh?'; and, if our imagination can supply us with the answer, so hard to find how we, in our circumstances, can apply just that advice to ourselves. But with St. Ignatius it is quite simple. Roughly speaking, you may say there was only one piece of advice he ever gave to anybody, and that was, 'Go into retreat.' He cries to us still, like Mathathias of old, 'Everyone that hath a zeal for the law, and maintaineth the Testament, let him follow me'; for our age, more than ever, that message holds good, if we are to save the world, if we are to save our souls.

XIV

St. Philip Neri

(Preached at Birmingham, to the Oratory School)

We are fools for Christ's sake (1 Cor 4:10).

I N UTTERING the praises of the Saints, it is possible to
concentrate your whole attention on the few features
of character that seem to be dominating, essential features,
and rule out of your considerations all that is second and
subsidiary to these as of no real importance. In doing so,
you assure yourself of an excellent moral; the only thing
is that the farther you proceed the more conscious you
become that your Saint is beginning to look exactly like
everybody else's Saint—the same mortifications, the same
abandonment of love, the same gifts in prayer. And at the
end of your task you have little left but a panegyric of St.
N., which you can easily use for St. Gregory the Great
one week and St. Margaret Mary the next. Now, if such a
study be your aim, there could be no Saint who satisfied
more minutely all the tests of holiness than St. Philip. If
an outside enquirer wanted a book which would explain
to him what sort of person you meant by a Saint, you certainly could not do better than refer him to Father Bacci.
But there is about St. Philip something so personal, so
intimate, so encouraging of familiarity, that devotion in
his case runs away from common themes and edifying

generalizations, and claims the right to busy itself rather with what was singular and characteristic about him than with the vital secret of his sanctity.

I do not mean simply his extraordinary humanness. It is quite true; his figure stands out to us, after all these centuries, as something very near and very natural to us. He is 'the Saint of gentleness and kindness'; 'love is his bond, he knows no other fetter, asks not our all, but takes whate'er we spare him': whatever difference of temperament there might be, the greatest of his English sons has not misinterpreted him. He is fond of animals. He likes to have boys around him, and does not mind how much noise they make if he can keep them from sin—a mortification which, perhaps, it takes a schoolmaster to appreciate. He fishes for souls with the line, not merely with the net; each penitent is, to him, an individual soul to be wooed and won, not a fresh case to be pigeon-holed. His portraits let you see him; nay, you can almost hear the cheerful 'What's up? What's up?' with which he greets his company. I suppose the simplest way of putting it into a phrase is to say that if you were alone in your room and the door opened and one of the Saints walked in, if it were almost any other you would fall on your knees, but if it were St. Philip you would run to his heart.

But there is one special element in that humanness which marks out Philip still more clearly from his heavenly compatriots: I mean his fun. You hear in the Middle Ages of God's minstrels or our Lady's troubadours, but I think it was left for the Counter-Reformation to produce that still more startling combination, God's jesters. We have one of them, thank God, in England, St. Thomas

More. There was nothing pleased him so much as the
reflection that if you put his name into Greek it meant a
fool. He was, perhaps, the only Saint who kept a private
jester as an honoured, almost a reverenced member of his
household. He carried off his sanctity (which, surely, was
there long before he won his crown by martyrdom) in
a cloud of raillery, and went to the scaffold joking, not
like a man who has screwed himself up to it, but like a
man bubbling over with irrepressible amusement. And St.
Philip has, as we all know, something of this same character. I do not mean his delightful habit of self-depreciation,
in which he has few parallels except, perhaps, the Curé
d'Ars. No, I mean that real, rollicking fun of St. Thomas
More, effervescing, in our Saint, in the form of the most
reckless practical jokes, played, now on himself, now on
his spiritual children. There is no denying it, is there?
Why, one of the first fathers of the Oratory confessed to
having wondered whether St. Philip were not touched
in the head, and St. Philip, in one of his most glorious
flights of holy fooling, made the poor man confess it in
refectory. No, we cannot get out of it, it is certainly there;
St. Philip is always dancing in public, or changing hats
with somebody, or making his penitents put their coats
on inside out; the fact cannot be disputed.

And of course we all know—our aunts, I suppose, did
not let us forget it when we were small—that the laughter
of fools is like the crackling of thorns under a pot, and a
loud laugh betrays an empty mind. Laughter, it is quite
true, is a difficult thing to find a warrant for in Scripture.
It is quite true that St. Philip always joked in public and
because he was in public; quite true that his jokes always

produced a holy fruit of mortification. In a full church, he went up to the Suisse or beadle at the church door and pulled his beard. I suppose none of us, in entering a foreign cathedral, can fail to be conscious of a temptation to do that: the point is that we are restrained by the fear of looking fools and the fear of hurting the beadle's feelings—precisely the two reasons why St. Philip did it. He succeeded in making the bystanders think the worse of him, and I suppose he succeeded in inflicting a salutary mortification on the beadle, though Father Bacci, to the annoyance of his readers, does not say what followed. But the laughter was there, and if it had not been there would have been no mortification; if everybody had kept his face who would have minded? I do not suppose St. Philip pulled the beard really hard. No, St. Philip really believed in ragging, and believed in it as a means to attaining the salvation of souls.

And I do not think it is any good saying that this was part of Philip's natural temperament, which came out in spite of his sanctity. I find no evidence for that; his early years are much like those of other Saints. No, it is a part of his sanctity; somehow, in those long vigils at the Catacombs, he had found out a secret; and that secret, for all his wonderful gift of tears, for all the miraculous palpitation of a heart love-sick for God, was one that could at times be communicated, could at times best be communicated to others, as a kind of celestial joke. The Holy Innocents, you would think, had been whispering in his ear. And he proceeded, not with a deep, artificial design, but, as St. Philip did everything, with complete naturalness and spontaneity, to make a fool of himself for Christ's sake.

Of course, if you were to ask which was nearer to the Saint's real interior life, his gift of tears or his gift of laughter, no one could hesitate in answering that it was his gift of tears. But the gift of tears is one which God, in his mercy, has granted to many others; the laughter is a more special feature, a more isolated characteristic. Will it, then, be a waste of time to try and see what it was that gave the edge to Philip's sense of merriment as he moved about in this valley of Divine chastisement and of human tears? I do not say that we shall be able to see the joke, if I may put it in that way; but it might be good for us even to understand what it was.

I say it may be hard for us to see it, because after all it is a joke against you and me and the world in general, and it is not always easy to see a joke when it is against yourself. There is, I suppose, no form of the ridiculous which has such a direct appeal as a situation in which somebody is putting on dignified airs, and all the time there is some circumstance, unknown to him but clearly seen by his audience, which makes that dignity absurd. You have come down without a tie, or somebody has written DONKEY on your back; and not only is your dignity unavailing but actually, the more dignity you assume, the more irresistibly funny you look—to those who can see. Now, the Saint who has been with God, who has familiarized himself with the thought of God's greatness and the heavenly scale of values—what must he think when he comes back to the unreal pomps, the sordid competition, the pretentious would-be wisdom of the world's citizens? Must not he see man as a coxcomb, strutting about in borrowed plumes, and making himself ridiculous afresh with every fresh air he puts on of proprietorship or of self-assertion? Must not he see the world's mad competition as a fond striving for prizes not worth the dust of conflict, and only capable of deluding us because we never rest satisfied with their attainment, but press on at once after others no less transitory? Oh, yes, I grant you, the cynic equally gets that point of view, but the cynic has only found the moral from the record of his own disappointments, and his heart is soured and warped, so that he may scourge the world with satire, but cannot save it from itself. But the Saint, the man whose heart is all on fire with desire for the salvation of his fellow-men, yet reads in the world about him the pathetic story of their misdirected effort: who sees the mockery of man's boasting, the futility of his striving, yet knows that Man, so ridiculous in his parade of earthly circumstance, is really a prince, if he but knew it, only not here—will not he be privileged to greet man's follies with the kindly laughter which has in it an echo of heaven and, with the infectiousness of that laughter, teach Man to know his present littleness, and through his littleness the greatness that might be his?

Sanctity, St. Philip used to say, rests within the compass of three inches; and he would point to his forehead to shew that what he meant was the mortification of the *razionale*, the proper pride that is perfection's most fatal enemy. And he knew that if he could get a penitent to laugh at himself—especially if worldly circumstances

made it natural for him to think too highly of himself—
that laugh, under God's Providence, would be the salvation of his soul. And he knew that there was one man
who, but for God's grace, was in hourly danger of falling
into a fatal self-satisfaction over the greatness of the revelations vouchsafed to him, and that man was Philip Neri
—very well, then, Philip Neri must be relentlessly pur-
sued with ridicule, must not pass a day without being
made to look silly. Yes, of course there was the need of
edifying others, but . . . of the people that come to be
edified, how large a proportion are really in earnest, how
many are merely sightseeing? Some Polish nobles to see
him? No, they are not really wanting to be edified; come
on, down with the detective stories, and let us be found
reading them to one another. . . . How like St. Philip!
And, if I may be pardoned for saying so, how Oratorian!

But, you will say, you have not recommended any of
his virtues to our imitation, for surely this playfulness
of his is the last thing we can afford to copy. No, I am
not suggesting ways in which we could imitate St. Philip,
but I think there is a quite practical lesson for our own
advancement. Suppose you went into one of these Con-
fessionals, and found the Saint himself sitting there; suppose that, won over by that invitation so few could resist, you opened to him (if he had not opened it already
to you) your whole heart—try to think what advice he
would give. What humiliating penance would he impose?
In what strange garb would he make you walk through
the streets of Birmingham? What cherished calculations
of self-interest would he dispel with that patient, insis-
tent question: 'Yes, and then . . . ?' 'Yes, and then . . . ?'

They are not distant historical figures, these Massimis and Tarugis you read of in the life; they are men of the same fashion with us, with our temptations, our difficulties. Can we not learn to read in their story the needs of our own souls?

Reverend Fathers, you cannot keep St. Philip to yourselves. The plant of devotion, which seemed so exotic when first you imported it into England from beneath Italian skies, has become acclimatized to our northern region, and springs self-sown in our hedgerows. He sees, I do not doubt, other temptations in our hearts beyond what he read in the hearts of his own penitents, but surely none that his example cannot arm us against, or his prayers cannot remedy. May those prayers being health to us who here celebrate his memory, and to all our countrymen, however little they have felt that influence till now, the graces they need for their eternal salvation.

XV

St. Charles Borromeo

(Preached at St. Mary of the Angels', Bayswater)

A great tempest arose in the sea, so that the boat was covered with waves, but he was asleep (Mt 8:24).

I T IS a common way of speaking in the Old Testament Scriptures to describe Almighty God as sleeping and awaking from sleep. When Israel is at the mercy of its enemies, and prayer and sacrifice is vain, when there is no voice and no answer of any that regards, then, by a natural metaphor, the Jew tells himself that God is asleep. He watching over Israel slumbers not, nor sleeps—that is the habitual confidence of Israel's faith. But when persecution arises, that confidence begins to vanish: 'Awake, Lord, why sleepest thou? Awake, and be not absent from us for ever'; and when deliverance comes, 'the Lord awaked as one out of sleep.' And you will find that in some of our Lord's parables Almighty God is compared to a householder who slept—it is the same idea: wickedness flourishes on the earth, and Divine Providence seems to take no notice, seems unwilling to interfere. So I imagine that when our Lord's Apostles came to look back upon that terrible night in the Lake of Galilee, when they strained every nerve against the tempest while their Master lay sleeping in the boat, they found in it an allegory of their own situation, as they launched out the frail bark of his Church upon waves so troubled, with prospects so uncertain. And in every age the Church has looked back to that picture and taken comfort from it in times of adversity: 'Yes, our Master seems to sleep; he gives no sign, vouchsafes no apparent answer to our prayers: no matter, we are safe from shipwreck, for he is still in our midst.'

When Julius Cæsar wished to cross from Durazzo to Brindisi in a little boat, and the master of it wanted to turn back, because the wind had risen and he was in danger of shipwreck, Cæsar rebuked him for his cowardice in noble words that have come down to us: 'Take courage, my friend, take courage, and fear nothing; Cæsar is your passenger, and Cæsar's fortunes are your freight.' With greater, and with better grounded confidence, the Church of God, which is Peter's boat, has breasted the waves all through her troubled history. It is not upon the captain's judgement or the pilot's experience, not upon human wisdom or human prudence, that she depends for her safe voyage: she rests secure in the presence of her inviolable passenger. Yet we should do ill if we grudged recognition and gratitude to those servants of his who at various times have steered our course for us through difficult waters, and especially to the Saints of the Counter-Reformation —that remarkable group of Saints whom God raised up at the time of Europe's apostasy, by whose influence, humanly speaking, the faith survived that terrible ordeal. And not the least, nor the least prominent, of these is your holy patron, who ruled the Church of Milan in the latter part of the sixteenth century.

Say what you will, Italy breeds the genius for government. So the greatest of Latin poets saw, and summed it up for us in a phrase:

> Others shall quicken bronze with softer grace,
> And from dull marble life's own features trace;
> Plead with more eloquence, the changing skies
> Map with more skill, and con the stars that rise:
> Roman, not these thy arts;—thy agelong skill
> To wield thy empire o'er the peoples still.

Anybody, in naming the world's great men, will give you almost at once the names of two Italians, Julius Cæsar and Napoleon. And, whatever verdict history may pass on our own times, it is in Italy that the anarchical tendencies of the last half-century have provoked the first reaction in favour of efficient government. St. Charles came from a ruling family among that ruling race. Personal humility shone out in him as in the other Saints; but there was something Latin all the same about the resolute competence with which he governed his diocese. Men called him a second St. Ambrose; and St. Ambrose, his predecessor in the See of Milan, was a civil magistrate before he was ever a bishop. It was no idle title to call St. Charles a prince of the Church.

Whatever be the rights and wrongs of all the controversies we hear about the medieval Church, this at least is clear, that in the days of the Council of Trent its organization needed reform. And reform needs more than mere legislation to decree it; it needs administration to execute it. That is St. Charles' characteristic legacy to the Church: it was the influence of his example, in great measure, that moulded her organization on the new model which Trent had decreed. The bishop has got to be the centre of everything in his diocese, and the clergy of the diocese are to be *his* clergy—a family of which he is to be the father, a guild of which he is to be the master. See how fond St. Charles was of synods: the whole of his comparatively short episcopate is a long record of the synods he gathered amongst his clergy. See how enthusiastic he is for the seminary idea; the bishop, henceforth, is not merely to ordain people, he is to know whom he is ordaining. And above all what was characteristic of St. Charles was the institute which he left behind him—a body of secular priests, putting themselves at the disposal of the bishop as absolutely as the religious puts himself at the disposal of his superior. Yes, there is much about St. Charles' life which is more exciting, and much which is more attractive, than all this; his boundless generosity to the poor, the relentless mortification that regulated his busy, competent life. But what makes him stand out among the Saints more than either is his intense devotion even to the most uninspiring details of diocesan routine.

In this church, where St. Charles' own spiritual children minister to you, something of his influence must surely impart itself to you; there must be some response in your blood to the appeal, long strange to our countrymen, of 'the Roman line, the Roman order.' And it is only right that the faithful who worship here should have a special devotion to ecclesiastical authority, and to the expression of that principle in the archdiocese of Westminster. It is the aim of a decent Catholic to obey his superiors; it is the aim of a good Catholic to obey his superiors lovingly. The virtue of obedience, nowadays, is a specifically Catholic virtue. The Protestant or half-believing or unbelieving world around us does not understand that it is a virtue at all. English people by temperament, by habit, by tradition, regard obedience as a tiresome necessity. Useful as training, perhaps, for schoolboys or for soldiers, but not a virtue in itself. The Protestant, in fact, thinks that obedience exists because without it there could be no authority. The Catholic is more likely to tell you that authority exists because without it there would be no obedience. The Catholic admits, quite as much as the Protestant, that man ought to realize himself, to develop every side of his nature, as far as he can do so without sin. But he sees also that the faculty for paying cheerful obedience to the orders of a human superior is one side of a man's nature, and if he never recognizes a human superior, that faculty will go undeveloped. It is a good thing, says the *Imitation*, to be under obedience to a prelate, and not to be one's own master—a good thing, not a convenient thing or a necessary thing, but something good in itself, a source of merit.

You see, when your Protestant sits down, if he ever does, to read the biography of a man like St. Charles, he says: 'Ah, yes, that is where these Catholics have the advantage! These crafty ecclesiastical statesmen, who treat every human agent they employ merely as a pawn in the game, who always sees exactly what each man is fitted for, and where he will be most use, that is where the power of the Catholic Church lies! The Vatican issuing its orders to the bishop, and the bishops to their clergy, every one of whom is simply a cog in a great machine! These seminaries, of course, turn all the priests out on a mould, and when they come out of them the bishop can play his crafty game of chess with them, and the thing is done. A triumph of organization, but hardly suited to the English mind or to modern circumstances.' That is the sort of picture of the Church which our obliging neighbours have invented for themselves in order to explain the fact that the Catholic Church is successful. We know that is a fable: we know that you have only got to live in the Catholic Church for a little in order to get the atmosphere of it, which is something totally different from that. But the Protestants are right about one thing; they are right in seeing that we have a tradition and a theory of obedience which they do not understand. Only it is not the obedience of blind tools that have lost all independence and all initiative. It is a submissiveness which we imitate from our Lady herself—*Ecce ancilla Domini!* It is a free act of loyalty by which Catholics acknowledge and accept the administrative authority of the Church, and hear in the commands of their superiors the voice of Almighty God.

And above all, Catholic obedience rallies to the person of that Supreme Pontiff, who holds his succession from the Pilot of the Galilean lake. With good omen, in these troubled times, we have seen a successor of St. Charles in Milan elevated to the throne of St. Pius the Fifth. In the present disintegration of Europe, that recalls to Catholic memory the storms of the sixteenth century, yet with cross-winds and cross-currents that are all its own, let us pray that the spirit of those two great Saints may unite in their successor, as he grasps the tiller of Peter's boat, and finds, God be thanked, that she still answers her helm. And let us renew our own loyalty to his person and to his office, determined that those instruments of Government which the Saints of the Counter-Reformation perfected, shall not through our fault lose their edge or be baulked of their purpose, the glory of Almighty God. To whom be praise and dominion for ever. Amen.

XVI

The English Martyrs

They that upset the world are come hither also (Acts 17:6).

WE ENTER this evening upon the Feast of the Invention of the Holy Cross, and to-morrow its relics will be exposed for veneration all over the world. Did you ever reflect, as you knelt before one of those chips of wood, upon its early history? Its history, I mean, before it became the instrument of our salvation. We have no record of its origin; in what forest the tree grew, or for what end it was first cut, or how it came to be brought to Jerusalem. Two planks, I suppose, lying about somewhere, and a soldier, the handy man of the legion, would fix them roughly together; not quite straight, perhaps, not quite true, but 'after all,' he would say to himself, 'it is good enough for what it has got to do.' A careless piece of carpentry, one of three jobs that had to be done by next morning, and in a hurry, because the need for it was unforeseen. And to-morrow a mere splinter of that wood, such as a man might run into his hand, will draw thousands of worshippers to their knees.

It is curious, is it not? Yet hardly more curious than the collection that is kept in this building; fragments of human bones and hair, patches of coarse cloth, shreds of linen with some dark stain on it. . . . Can you imagine what a stranger from some other planet would make of it, a man, if such were possible, without any idea or conception of God? You would persuade him that the collection was not one of mere odds and ends; that a certain interest attached to these things merely from the historical fact of their having been in contact with men of times past, the victims of a series of judicial murders. 'Yes,' he would say, 'but, even so, is it not rather morbid? Is not one Chamber of Horrors enough for you people in London? Surely it is a perverted instinct in our nature that makes a story of crime so thrilling to us, that brings out a crowd on a cold morning just to see a flag hoisted when some murderer in a prison forfeits to justice the life he has misused; that throngs the inquest, and hardly allows the ambulance to pass? It is well to feed this unnatural taste by keeping alive in perpetuity the trophies of a tyranny that has long since passed?' And we should try to tell him about the martyrs, and what they mean to us. And he would still persist: 'Yes, but are you not making much of that very thing of which the martyrs themselves made so light? They handed over their bodies to the tormentor precisely because their bodies were of no account in comparison to their immortal souls; and you, in your ghoulish treasure-chambers, hoard up the very trappings of mortality they despised. Did not St. Thomas More, as you call him, move his beard aside from the block because *that* had not committed treason? The soul, surely, not the body, is what matters. Cannot you bury the bodies of your Saints in peace, and be content that their name should live for evermore?'

What answer should we make? I suppose this: That we do not treasure these relics as men treasure the ghastly evidences of some atrocious crime, but rather as the trophies of a conquest; we gather these bones as you might gather the droppings of some precious metal that had been tried in the fire, we catch the drops of blood as if it were some rare vintage flowing from the wine-press. If a housebreaker gave us the choice whether he should steal one of these bones, or the golden reliquary that enshrines it, we should, without affectation, resign the reliquary as a thing of smaller worth. We put a different value on these historical events from those around us. These men, you see, were the men who upset the world. And for us, their children, the world is still topsy-turvy, and the meaning of things and the values of things are stated, for us, in terms of a new currency. To us death is life, and defeat is victory. I love that phrase, used of the Apostles, 'these men that upset the world'—so much so, I am afraid, that I have taken the liberty of translating it as it stands in the Greek original, although the present text of our Latin Bible, by an obvious slip which I have no doubt the Pontifical Commission will set right, has represented St. Jerome as writing Urbem, the city, instead of Orbem, the world. To upset the world—it is the word that's used to describe the depopulating of a conquered country, when the victor turns everybody out of house and home and pulls down their roof-trees about their ears. The martyrs are the people who have done that to the whole world. Whenever we feel inclined to turn round and settle down and feel really comfortable in this world of our pilgrimage, the example of the martyrs is there to evict us and make us feel uncomfortable once more. God's Saints don't content themselves with overcoming the world, they are determined to make the place quite uninhabitable for you and me. That is the boast of our religion; it's also the reason why some people dislike it.

But I am going ahead too fast; let us tell our strange visitor who these martyrs were and what were the circumstances of this deplorable miscarriage of justice. The question which sent St. Thomas More and St. John Fisher, whom we commemorate especially at this time, to their deaths, was the question whether they would take or refuse an oath which recognized the validity of an adulterous union contracted by their sovereign; the preamble to which oath—only the preamble—cast aspersions on the right of the Holy See to judge (as it did judge, in a contrary sense) matters of this character. This was long before any considerable body of people in England had contemplated the possibility of being anything other than Catholics. To the mass of men, even to devoted Catholics, even to the martyrs' best friends and kinsmen, the refusal of the oath seemed a scruple, an exaggeration of conscience. Could not a man take the oath without committing himself to all the bad doctrine that might be contained in the preamble? Was it even wise to force an issue between the monarchy and the Papacy? Do not let us blame the people who argued like that. They could not see, as we can see now, what this defiance of ecclesiastical authority was to lead to. The Chancellor, in criticizing St. Thomas More's conduct, said it reminded him of a fable of Æsop about a country where it was prophesied that a strange rain was about to fall, which would turn everybody it wetted into fools. All the wisest men hid themselves when it came, and expected afterwards to be able to have the fools at their mercy, but found instead that the fools persisted in governing themselves their own way, and they would have been wiser still to stay out in the rain and be turned into fools like the rest of them. It was true; the minds of the generality of men had been blinded, and the few wise men who had escaped that infection must either resign their sane opinions or pay for them with their lives.

But there were such people. The upsetters of the world had come hither also; had come even to England, to upset things just when everybody was going to be comfortable. They had that awkward, subversive temperament which sees everything upside down, which measures life only as the ante-chamber of death, time only as the preface to eternity. St. Thomas More really could not see that he was any worse off in the Tower than at Chelsea; they were both equally close to heaven. And yet this was a man to whom his home was a sort of Paradise, who would have been unwilling, you would think, to spend a day out of reach of his library! He has learned, somehow, to measure things by the standard of eternity, and the peace of his own soul really does mean more to him than the peace of his country. He deliberately breaks up our home, our comfortable home, the world.

We do not forget, and God forbid that we should forget, the cause for which our martyrs died. Because the faith for which they suffered persecution was their faith in the privileges divinely conferred upon the Holy See, it is for us, their clients and their fellow-countrymen, to be distinguished, if there must be such distinction, above the other nations of the world by our whole-hearted devotion to the Vicar of Christ. So much is due in expiation for the sins of our forefathers, in gratitude for the testimony borne by our holy patrons. But it is not for us to perpetuate by letting the grim memories of past wrongs rankle in our minds, our personal quarrel with the Protestantism which sent the martyrs to their death. Bear a grudge against the Church of England for events that happened nearly four centuries ago? Believe me, it would be an unnecessary compliment. For the church which—in some of its utterances—claims continuity with the Christendom of Augustine and Dunstan, cannot even claim the credit of continuity with itself. The Christianity which we see around us has little to do, for better or for worse, with the Christianity of the sixteenth century divines. Brought up in the breezy historical tradition of Charles Kingsley and the smaller Gardiner, it leaves the record of the martyrs a forgotten page in history. Well, in the face of that forgetfulness, it is good indeed that we should do everything to tend the memory of our martyrs, and to make public display of our devotion, but it should be with no feelings of resentment towards the mutilated Christianity which the evil tradition of the persecutors has left to our fellow-countrymen. For, after all, what the martyrs triumph over is not the fury of the persecutor, it is the spell of the things which persecution takes from them: they triumph over the attractiveness of peace, of ease, of liberty, of comfort, of companionship, of health, and finally—the greatest attraction of all—of life itself. You do not tremble, when you read the story of St. Thomas

More confronting his judges, lest he should be brow-beaten or bullied into surrender. But you do catch your breath just a little for fear heaven should lose a martyr, when wife and daughter, not of any ill intent, but with misplaced affection, come to dissuade him from his holy purpose. A smaller man might have resisted the efforts of a Cromwell; it needed the martyr's heroism to resist the appeals of Margaret Roper. If we are to learn to imitate St. Thomas More, we shall not do it by despising Protestants; we shall do it by despising Chelsea. It is the world that the martyrs trample under their feet; it is the world they would have us triumph over as best we may.

Of this attitude of defiance towards the world our English Catholicism ought, from the very circumstances of its past, to be a continual reminder. It is a matter of historical atmospheres. To have had the experience of teaching —if you will pardon my being autobiographical—in an Oxford College founded by Sir Thomas Pope, who was actually St. Thomas More's gaoler in the Tower; to have gone on to teach at a school which acknowledged as its chief benefactors King Edward the Sixth and Queen Elizabeth; and then, as a Catholic, to find yourself teaching at the very college founded by an exiled Cardinal for the training of seminary priests for England in the time of the persecution—that change means, so far as your historical perspective is concerned, a complete change of values. To have been brought up among the busts of portly gentlemen in semi-classical costume who became Lord Chancellors and Poets Laureate and what not, people who started as boys with your hopes, your ambitions, and succeeded, one way and another, in scrambling up the difficult slopes

of fame, among portraits of Bishops with puffy sleeves
and lawyers in important wigs; and then to find yourself
in a place where the most treasured roll of school suc-
cesses is a long list of names the world has never heard
of, men who died convicted as traitors to their country
—that should be, to anybody, a sufficiently impressive
sermon on the rewards to be sought in this world and
in the next. I was taught where, we are assured on good
authority, the battle of Waterloo was won. I am teaching
where the battle of Tyburn was won, and I thank God
for it.

Oh, how they upset the world for us, these martyrs
of ours, or if they do not, how they ought to upset it
for us! Where we seek our gratification, they found their
mortification; they blessed the discomforts we repine at,
spurned the crowns we pant for, flicked their fingers at
the master that so easily whistles us to heel—human respect. To us, eternity is a mere background, sketched in
dimly behind this life, the central incident on our mind's
canvas. To them, the picture was the landscape of eternity; the figures of this world were merely dotted about in
the foreground to give value to the rest. And at Tyburn,
whether it be the influence of their prayers or the continuous miracle of the Eucharistic Presence, I cannot say,
but there is a spirit that communicates to those who offer
their prayers in this place something of that other worldly
focus. The wheels hum and the motors hoot and the cries
of the street fall on your ear, but, praying here before the
monstrance, you know, somehow, that this, not that, is
the reality, here, not there, is the true current of human

endeavour. We, too, if only for the moment, feel that we could endure like the martyrs as seeing him who is invisible, that amidst the world's changefulness our hearts could there be set, where are the true joys. For a moment we really see the world as the puppet-show it is.

Let us praise God, then, for our English martyrs, Thomas More and John Fisher and the Charterhouse monks, and, from Blessed Cuthbert Mayne onward, the long line of proscribed and hunted priests. Men of our blood, they have left sayings which ring more familiarly to us than the translated pieties of the Continent; men of our latter-day civilization, they stand out with more of human personality than the mist-wreathed heroes of the medieval world. And surely, if they have not forgotten among those delights of eternity the soft outlines and the close hedgerows and the little hills of the island that gave them birth; if in contemplating the open face of God, they have not ceased to take thought for the well-loved kingdom that exiled and disowned them, the patiently evangelized people that condemned and hurried them to the gallows, their prayers still rise especially, among all the needs of a distracted world, for the souls we love whom error blinds or sin separates from God. It is Mary's month; we hardly dare, so wide are the sympathies of her immaculate Heart, to think of our country as singled out in her intercessions: yet we are her dowry, and while the world lies suppliant at her feet she will not forget the triduum we keep in these first days of May. God grant that through the power of such intercessors, whatever unworthiness and degeneracy he sees in us English Catholics of a later day may be pardoned and set aside, and that our brethren, so long sought, so patiently wooed by the Divine grace, may return to the allegiance of the true Church, and make England a shrine of martyrs and a nursery of Saints once more.

XVII

The Oxford Martyrs

(Preached at the Undergraduates' Chaplaincy)

Remember the days of old; think upon every generation (Deut 32:7).

Y OU WILL probably have seen in the papers this week,
if you did not know it before, that the claim of
some two hundred and fifty of our fellow-countrymen to
the honours of martyrdom are now being considered at
Rome; and that a large number of them, some two hundred in all probability, are likely to be beatified either this
month or in the very near future. By a fortunate accident,
the feast of the Oxford martyrs, which we celebrate in
this archdiocese, falls this year on a Sunday, this Sunday.
The whole total of the English martyrs, if you include
those who have already been beatified, is three hundred
and fifteen; and in view of the historical circumstances
it is not a little remarkable that exactly one-fifth of these
were Oxford men. No less than seventeen colleges are
represented out of a possible twenty. It would be out of
place, I think, to go over the old ground of controversy
and remind ourselves once more how monstrous was the
attempt of politicians, and later of historians, to brand the
great majority (at least) of these names with the stigma of
treason. Instead of that, I thought I would just give you a

few thumb-nail biographies, if I may so call them, of a few among these many; and I have chosen, for that purpose, the names of those Oxford men who have already been beatified, and who suffered as seminary priests in the earlier years of Queen Elizabeth's reign, before the Spanish Armada. This selection will reduce the whole number to a dozen or so; we have hardly time for more.

You must begin any such list with the Jesuit, Blessed Edmund Campion. He was one of the original scholars of St. John's when it was founded in 1555; he became public orator of the university and junior proctor. He was generally regarded as *the* Oxford man of his period, and Queen Elizabeth herself was delighted with his eloquence. But of course he enjoyed all this fame under a miserable condition; he had to take the oath of supremacy, and was ordained deacon according to the ritual of the Protestant Prayer-book. He thought, perhaps, as many have thought since his time, that he could do better work for the Catholic cause by 'staying where he was.' Like Newman, he exercised an extraordinary influence over the minds of others; like Newman, he must have felt that his choice lay between Oxford and Rome. He left Oxford, and went over to Dublin, still as a Protestant; but his conscience was being too strong for him, and after witnessing the trial of Blessed John Story in London he went abroad, first to Douai, and then to Rome, where he entered the society. He worked first in Bohemia; then was sent to the English mission, and, among other vast apostolic labours, printed his 'Ten Reasons' at a secret printing press. He was apprehended at Lyford Grange, near Wantage; was offered life and preferment by the Queen herself if he would return to Protestantism; was mercilessly racked, and finally, by an afterthought, condemned on a ridiculous charge of treason. He suffered at Tyburn on this day, in the year 1581.

St. John's also claims the first martyr among the secular clergy, Blessed Cuthbert Mayne. He was educated by his uncle, a priest who had conformed to the new religion. He was apparently already ordained when he came up, first to St. Alban's Hall—that is, for practical purposes, to Merton—and then to St. John's, where he took his M.A. in 1570. In the same year, when he was already considering the question of his religious allegiance, like other members of Campion's circle, a letter addressed to him from abroad fell into the wrong hands; he disappeared from Oxford, and we next meet him in 1573, at Douai, where he was ordained, and sent back to England in 1576. He worked in Cornwall, where he passed as the steward of a well-to-do Catholic; but after a year of this the pursuivants found him, and he was led off to trial. No charge was brought against him which could be supposed to have any political bearing whatsoever. One of the judges protested against his sentence, and the case had to be remitted to London; the Government simply ordered his execution, and he was murdered on November 29, 1577.

When Sir William Petre extended the foundation of Exeter in 1565, one of the first scholars he nominated was Ralph Sherwin, who took his degree there in 1574, and was reckoned an accomplished scholar both in Greek and in Hebrew. By the next year he, too, had left for Douai. Not much is known of his life, and he was apprehended when he had only been on the mission for about half a year. But the story of his imprisonment, of his twice-repeated torture on the rack, and of the five days during which he lay without food or drink, and found at the end of them 'no distemper in his joints by reason of his racking' are among the most noteworthy of our martyrs' records. He should also be remembered for some of his last utterances; it was he who, after his condemnation, pointed up at the sun and said: 'I shall soon be above yon fellow'; he who said on the scaffold: 'If to be a Catholic only be to be a traitor, then I am a traitor'; he who died with the words 'Jesu, Jesu, Jesu, esto mihi Jesus.' He was martyred at the same time as Blessed Edmund Campion.

In 1574 a strikingly handsome young man came up to Hert Hall, which we now call Hertford. His name was Alexander Briant; he came from Somersetshire, where the old faith had died hard. It was a Somersetshire man, Robert Persons, who was afterwards a member of the Society of Jesus and one of the most active, if not always one of the most discreet, partisans of the Catholic cause in England. Persons was then a fellow of Balliol, and young Briant was his pupil, so that he must have been early attracted towards the Catholic cause. He must have gone down without taking his degree, for by the year 1578 he had already gone out to Douai and been ordained priest there. He returned to England, and went back to his own county of Somerset, to reconcile heretics and minister to Catholics. Among others he reconciled the father of his old Oxford tutor. When he was apprehended, as he very soon was, he had to suffer for this connexion; the Government were particularly anxious to lay

hands on Persons, who was then himself in England, and
they tortured Alexander Briant unmercifully in the hope
of information, driving needles, for example, between his
finger-nails and fingers. Soon before his martyrdom, he
applied for and was granted admission into the Society of
Jesus. He suffered with Campion and Sherwin, on this
day, at the age of twenty-eight.

For myself, I feel specially bound to pray to Blessed
Thomas Ford, fellow of Trinity in 1567. He was a Devonshire man, and perhaps as a Devonshire man he was
already acquainted with Cuthbert Mayne at St. John's; certainly it was he who warned Mayne of the danger threatening him when that letter from abroad went astray. Nor
was it long before he himself followed his friend abroad,
arriving at Douai in 1570. He took a long course at Douai,
and did not come back to England till 1576; he was sent to
work at Lyford Grange, not far from Abingdon—indeed,
it is not a dozen miles from where we sit; and it is clear
that there were close relations between the Catholics who
remained in Oxford, and the safe moated grange in Berk-
shire where they could go off to hear Mass. It was quite an
establishment that Mrs. Yate kept there; there were eight
Bridgettine nuns sheltered in her house. Then one day
there was great excitement in the little colony—Edmund
Campion was to pay them a visit. He came, stayed the
night, and left; then Thomas Ford had to ride after him
and bring him back, because a crowd of sixty or more,
from Oxford and elsewhere, had come over to hear him
preach. His return was fatal to him, and to Thomas Ford
as well; both of them, with another priest, were observed
by a spy and captured in a hiding-place where they had

taken refuge. So Thomas Ford shared the ignominious ride to London with Campion, and Campion's imprisonment; he was finally condemned on the accusation that he had taken part in a conspiracy, or an alleged conspiracy, in Rome and again at Rheims, during a time which he had, as a matter of fact, spent entirely in England. He was martyred some time after Campion, in 1582.

As Campion and Ford were being taken from Lyford to London, they were passing through a part of the country where the faith still had its strongholds, notably at Stonor Hall, near Henley. It was at Henley that another priest incautiously tried to speak with Campion, so giving himself away and being carried off with the others. This was William Filby, an Oxford martyr in a double sense; for he was a native of the town, and had been up as an undergraduate at Lincoln. He matriculated in 1575, and was at Rheims by 1579; there he was ordained, and must presumably have been sent to work in Oxfordshire, but as he was only ordained in 1581, the year of Campion's apprehension, he must have had a short missionary life. From the November of that year till the following May he was kept in handcuffs, and then executed at Tyburn.

Two other Oxford priests were executed with him, both from Brasenose. One of these, Laurence Richardson, was a Lancashire man, and not only came from Lancashire, still so largely Catholic, but from Great Crosby, still intimately connected with the name of a Catholic family. It seems pretty clear that he must have been a 'born Catholic,' as we say, and we may perhaps look upon him as a member of this congregation in a sense in which Edmund Campion and the others were not. Nevertheless he seems to have managed to take his degree; that was on November 25, 1573; and Challoner says that he was a fellow of the College, though Gillow seems to deny this: the family from which he came were recusants right up to 1717, and it seems hard to understand how he could conscientiously have taken a fellowship under the religious conditions of those times. In any case, he left Oxford almost immediately for Douai, where he was admitted in 1573. He returned as a priest, four years later, to Lancashire, and acted as chaplain at Ince Blundell—the Blundells were his cousins. In Lancashire persecution was not so easy to organize as in the south, but he was apprehended in London, and charged with complicity in the same plot in which Thomas Ford was supposed to have been involved, though he too had never left England during the time in question. He was martyred in 1582, repeating St. Stephen's words: Lord Jesus receive my soul.

The other Brasenose man who was martyred at the same time was, like Laurence Richardson, a man of good family, and came like him from Lancashire. His brother, who succeeded to the estates, appears on the recusants' rolls, but he, it seems, must have been reconciled to the Church, for the parents were Protestants. Thomas Cottam, therefore, will have come up as a Protestant; he took his degree in 1568, and then went off to teach at a grammar school in London. Here he was converted, and went abroad; his desire was, apparently, to join the Society of Jesus and go out to the Indian missions. His health prevented this, and he was ordained at Rheims in 1580. The moment he landed at Dover he was arrested, on the evidence of a spy who had met him abroad. Then an extraordinary thing happened. The Mayor of Dover gave him into the charge of a gentleman who was travelling to London, to be delivered into safe custody there. This gentleman was really a Catholic and a priest, Dr. Ely by name; and he insisted on Thomas Cottam going free when he got to London, though somewhat against his own conscience. Later, Dr. Ely was in danger of getting into trouble for not delivering up his prisoner, and Cottam voluntarily gave himself up to save the situation. He was taken to the Marshalsea and tortured; out of sheer wantonness, it would seem, because they did not try to extract any secrets from him. He was thirty-three when he went to his eternal reward.

The same college produced another of these martyrs, John Shert. He was a Cheshire man, and took his degree from Brasenose in 1566; like Cottam, he was for a time a schoolmaster in London, then went to Rheims, and came back to England in 1579. His work lay in London, and there for two years he managed to escape detection; he was then committed to the Tower, and condemned with Thomas Ford for the conspiracy which he, like Thomas Ford, knew nothing at all about; he, too, had been in England at the time alleged. He suffered immediately after Thomas Ford, to whom he boldly prayed on the scaffold as to one already in heaven.

Lincoln, too, has another beatified martyr, Blessed William Hart. He came from Somersetshire and caught the infection of Catholicism which still lingered in Oxford; went abroad to Douai and afterwards to Rome, and was ordained priest, it seems, when he was only twenty-one. He worked on the mission at York, where his charity and his eloquence made him almost a public figure; yet even in York, where sympathy with the old religion was still strong, he went in danger of his life, and on one occasion had to climb down the walls of the castle and hide in a moat to save his life. They arrested him on Christmas Day, 1582; and the charges at his trial were so frivolous that the foreman of the jury demanded to be dismissed, and had actually to be dismissed before a verdict was brought in against him. A most touching letter, written to his Protestant mother on the eve of his execution, has been preserved to us. He suffered in 1583.

Two months later, in the same city of York, they executed another Oxford martyr, Blessed Richard Thirkeld. He was up at Queen's in 1564–1565, but it is not known what became of him between that time and his ordination at Rheims, fourteen years later. He was a native of Durham, and when he came back to England he was stationed at York, where he was confessor to the well-known martyr, Margaret Clitheroe. He was one of those martyrs who have longed for martyrdom from the first; for eight years he had prayed for it. Accordingly, when he was arrested on York bridge and accused of being a priest, he immediately admitted it, instead of leaving it to his prosecutors to prove the charge. He actually appeared in court in his cassock and biretta; and he was condemned without difficulty on his willing confession that he had reconciled the Queen's subjects to their allegiance to the spiritual power of the Pope. When he was executed, the

Mayor of York held a general meeting of the citizens elsewhere, for enrolling the militia; so doubtful was the effect, in York, of public executions for religion.

Well, there are eleven martyrs for you. I have not included two Oxford martyrs who suffered under Elizabeth, Blessed Thomas Plumtree of Corpus, and Blessed
John Storey, master of Broadgates Hall (now Pembroke),
because although they suffered under Elizabeth they were
not seminary priests; they had been brought up at Oxford when it was still a centre of Catholic learning, before the death of King Henry the Eighth. Remember that
these names are only a fifth of those martyrs, beatified or
waiting to be beatified, whom Oxford numbers among
her sons; remember that the Oxford martyrs in their turn
have to be multiplied by five before you reach the total
of the English martyrs.

I am not going to draw any elaborate morals from what
I have told you. I would just draw your attention to the
ages of these men; I suppose their average age was about
thirty-one; they did not live long, and they knew that they
would not live long. When they were up at Oxford the
world was all at their feet, and a world which held out
greater opportunities, one would say, than our world, for
men who wanted to make a name and get the best out of
life. They could hope to become paragons of chivalry like
Sidney, courtiers like Raleigh, adventurers like Drake, poets like Spenser; or, if they were determined to embrace
a clerical career, there were easy openings for them, and
ample emoluments for them, in the Church of England.
But conscience beckoned them, and they gave up all that
prospect, to go and live in a little dusty Flemish town,

which promised them the life of an outlaw, and death at thirty-one.

They were our fellow-students; as they lay in prison, little vignettes of Oxford must have danced before them; the Cottages at Worcester, and Mob Quad at Merton, and Christ Church Hall, and Magdalen Tower, and New College cloisters, and the old library at Trinity, and the front of St. John's, were as familiar sights to them as to us who follow them; they must remember them still, if heaven is to be the completion of our life on earth. St. Silvester, whose feast we celebrated last Tuesday, was converted by the sight of a young man's corpse in an open grave; 'This man,' he said to himself, 'was what I am; what this man is, I shall be.' Let us take a kindred lesson from the martyrs of whom we have been speaking. They were what you are, Oxford undergraduates. God grant that you may be what they are, citizens of the kingdom of heaven.

XVIII

The Derby Martyrs

(Preached in the market square at Derby)

For we are the good odour of Christ unto God, in them
that are saved and in them that perish; to the latter indeed
the odour of death unto death, but to the former the odour
of life unto life (2 Cor 2:15–16).

ON JULY 24, 1588, at a moment when the Spanish Armada was cruising off the south coast, somewhere
between Plymouth and the Isle of Wight, three Catholic
priests were put to death in this town with the horrible
tortures then prescribed for those guilty of high treason.
Their offence, as usual, was a merely technical one, that
of being priests and celebrating Mass; there is no record
which suggests that they had been concerned with political activities. The name of the best known among these
three priests was Nicholas Garlick.

Garlick—it is not a pretty name. It reminds you, inevitably, of a class of plants with a very pungent smell,
which most of us dislike. And I have no doubt that on that
day of July, more than three hundred years ago, the street
boys of Derby made merry on the subject, holding their
noses, as likely as not, while Nicholas Garlick was drawn
on his hurdle to the gallows. They will have thought of
garlic as the name of a nasty scent; they will have forgotten that this plant, however distressing it may be to the

nostrils, has a high medicinal value. The smell of it may be deadly, but its properties are life-giving. If they had thought of that, their minds might perhaps have travelled back to another preacher of the Christian religion, fifteen centuries before; they might have remembered how he wrote to his friends in Corinth: 'We are the good odour of Christ; to them that perish, the odour of death unto death; but to them that are saved, the odour of life unto life.'

An odour of death unto death, an odour of life unto life—that means that the Christian message is what you make of it. If you find it deadly, then it is deadly, to you; if you find it life-giving, then it is life-giving, to you. I do not mean that at the time when our martyrs suffered, all those who took part in tormenting them, all those who joined in the cry against them and jested at them on their way to execution, involved themselves thereby in eternal damnation. The tendency to shout with the crowd is one of the strongest, and on the whole one of the most pardonable tendencies, in human nature; nor can there be much doubt, I suppose, that at the time of the Spanish Armada the English public was worked up into an attitude of intense antipathy to everything which it suspected of being foreign. Fear is a great promoter of cruelty. But I do say that when you read the history of the martyrs you will find in it an admirable illustration of how the doctrines of our holy religion, which seem, and are, so life-giving to us, can seem, and be (so far as their rejection is culpable), deadly to those who reject them.

An odour of death—the Catholic religion had already begun to seem, to the young people of that day, a dead thing, a back number, a page from the history of the past. Human memories are lamentably short; there must have been old folks in Derby who could remember the Old Religion well enough; who had seen, when they were young, the habits of the black monks and the black nuns, and had experience of their charity. But the younger people—remember that the Protestant religion had been in the saddle for thirty years. The days of Queen Mary were exactly as remote from them as the days of Queen Victoria are from us. If you think of all the changes that have come over England since 1901; if you think, for example, of the growth of the Labour Movement in these thirty years, that will give you some idea of how remote the Catholic religion must have appeared to the people who were just growing up and marrying at the time of the Spanish Armada.

These priests, then, these seminary priests who slunk about the town in their disguises, must have seemed to Englishmen of the day part of a dead world, like ghosts from the old graveyards which housed the bones of their Catholic ancestors. And yet there must have been old-fashioned people about the town, with their families, who had never accepted the new religion; had conformed to it outwardly, perhaps, through fear of consequences, but had never come to believe in the claims of the usurping ministers who occupied the parish pulpits. And to them, these seminary priests were an odour of life; they brought back memories of the old days when Mass was said at St. Alkmund's, when the figures, the emblems of our Lady and the Saints were to be seen everywhere, in a brighter and a freer England. In this dead world of Protestantism the sight of Father Garlick or Father Ludham, passing by them without recognition in the street, was like a ray of sunshine piercing through fog. For these men brought with them that Bread of Life which had been interdicted to a starving England these thirty years. An odour of life unto life.

An odour of death—how they must have marvelled, those ordinary Englishmen of the day, at the persistency with which priest after priest came back from the Continent to work on the English mission, only to fall after a year or two into the hands of the pursuivants, and atone for their heroism by death! These three priests of whom we are speaking had only been able to work for souls half a dozen years before they met their end; and in each case with an interval of banishment. How mad they must have thought us, to suppose that we were going to keep alive the embers of the old religion, when a seminary course of six years only qualified our priests for six years of apostolate! If ours was not a dead religion, at least ours was a dying body; a few years more, and it would be bound to come to an end, from sheer attrition of numbers. Poor Garlick, only another weed rooted out, as all the weeds must before long be rooted out, from the beautiful, ordered garden of Protestant England!

And yet—an odour of life; those others, those few who still clung to the faith of their ancestors recognized, with whatever doubts, with whatever failings of the heart, that this long pageant of butchery, so far from threatening the Catholic religion with extinction, was in reality deepening and widening its influence; that every judicial murder meant another martyr praying before the throne of

God for our apostate country, another model of fortitude, to encourage fresh souls to embrace the same hazardous career, another outrage, to sicken Englishmen at last of the brutal work. One after another, political hopes failed them; but they clung on, none the less jealously, to the tradition of their forefathers, and left a stock surviving to be fertilized in God's own time, and to grow and flourish beyond all the measure of their hopes.

Still doomed to death, and fated not to die—so wrote our Catholic poet of the faith he had embraced; and this has been, everywhere and at all times, its history. For it seems, our faith, a thing rooted in the past, wrapped up with a great deal of venerable imagery, of forgotten ceremony, of exploded tradition; so that even those who hate it will sometimes speak of it in tones of hushed respect, as men speak of the dead. But the fact is that it is alive; that in the midst of all this modern hurry and heedlessness of the past, all this frantic worship of to-morrow, our Church is attracting converts to itself as no other religious body in England is attracting them, is expanding its borders as no other religious body in England dares to expand them. It looked a dead thing compared with the Protestant religion which had superseded it, thirty years after Elizabeth came to the throne; to-day, thirty years after Queen Victoria ended her reign, does the same comparison survive? Is it not rather true that those who are frightened of us, and there are still many who are frightened of us, attribute those fears, openly, to the growth in Catholic numbers and Catholic influence which our generation has witnessed?

The Catholic Church always seems to despise all measures which would promote her own survival. She takes some of her most devout sons, and bids them follow, in the priesthood, a life of celibacy; she takes many of those women whom you would expect to become the mothers of pious Catholic families, and immures them in the cloister. You would say she was pursuing a policy of ecclesiastical race suicide. And yet in our own day, when parenthood has ceased to be held in honour, and thoughtful men are directing our attention to a decline in the birthrate, and the possibility that the English stock will die out, it is the Catholic body more than any other which is resisting that tendency and breeding the Englishmen of the next generation. It is the odour of life, not of death, that breathes from the Catholic Church, now as then.

Only, now as then, we Catholics have to keep alive among us that same spirit of devoted sacrifice in which the martyrs gave their lives for the Church. These are hard times all round, and we may well meet harder times before long; and we Catholics shall feel them not least, with the burden of large families and the burden of supporting our children's education. We shall grumble, sometimes, at the sacrifices demanded of us. But before we grumble, let us pause awhile on the old bridge and think of three men, Nicholas Garlick, Robert Ludham, and Richard Simpson, who were butchered there in cold blood, when times were worse than ours. God grant, through the prayers of all the English martyrs, that we ourselves may not be found wanting in whatever trials his mercy may suffer us to undergo.

XIX

Bernadette of Lourdes

Put off the shoes from thy feet, for the place whereon thou standest is holy ground (Ex 3:5).

ABOUT three thousand years ago, a man stood, thrilled with religious awe, on the slopes of Mount Sinai in Arabia. He was a shepherd, feeding on those barren pastures the flocks of his father-in-law; his attention had been aroused, at a distance, by the unwonted sight of a fire in the desert scrub. And now that he had drawn nearer, he saw that this was not merely something beyond the ordinary, but something beyond nature itself; the bush before which he stood burned continually, but was not consumed. At the same time a divine warning came to him that he must take off the shoes from his feet in sign of reverence. He did so, and when he had done so the Divine Voice came to him again; he was to bear a message to his brethren, the children of Israel, subject at that time to a barbarous captivity in Egypt. The God of their fathers, the God of Abraham and Isaac and Jacob, would deliver them from that bondage; and when they had come out of Egypt, they were to do sacrifice to him on this mountain of Sinai. And, in token of the new covenant he was to make with his people, the God of Abraham and Isaac and Jacob revealed himself by a new name: I AM WHO AM.

Rather less than eighty years ago, a little girl stood before the rock of Massabieille, in the township of Lourdes, on the slopes of the Pyrenees. No premonition of any divine event disturbed her thoughts; she was at play with her companions, and if she took off the shoes from her feet it was only to cross the stream that lay in their path. She heard a noise, like that of a strong wind; she turned, and saw that the trees in the valley were not bowed as a strong wind must bow them. She turned back towards the rock, and a rose-bush that grew in front of it. And now she saw the rose-bush flaming with something more bright, more pure, more beautiful than fire. She saw above it the figure of a Lady; what need to describe it in detail? Wherever Christendom reaches, the helpless aspirations of Christian artists have made that figure familiar to every human eye. The Lady said no word, but she made one sign, the Sign of the Cross; and the little girl, taking courage, said her rosary as if to defend her from harm. Then the Vision beckoned to her to come nearer; she drew back in alarm, and it vanished. She took off her other stocking, crossed the stream, and rejoined her companions, who had seen nothing. That was all; it was only in later visits that she realized what a grace had been bestowed upon her; that she, too, was to lead a world out of its captivity; draw it after her to worship God and celebrate the glories of his Mother on that mountain. It was only many days later that the gracious Lady revealed herself by name; lifted up her eyes to heaven and said: 'I am the Immaculate Conception.'

Moses was a shepherd, not by choice. A man of courts and palaces, he had been driven into exile, and served, in that exile, his apprenticeship among the flocks. It is curious how often God has chosen a shepherd when he has wanted to impart an inspiration that has revolution-ized men's lives. Jacob was a shepherd, the founder of the Jewish race; David was a shepherd, the ancestor of its royal dynasty; Amos was a shepherd, the first of its sons to prophesy and to commit his prophecies to writing. And under the new dispensation it is not otherwise; the shepherds at Bethlehem were the first to hear from their cronies, the Angels, of the Divine-Human Birth, and you will find shepherd Saints in every age of Christian piety —St. Geneviève, St. Paschal Baylon, St. Vincent de Paul, St. John Vianney. Curious, did we say? There is nothing curious about it when you come to think of it. For God himself was content to be described by his ancient people as a Shepherd; 'Hear, thou shepherd of Israel,' 'The Lord is my shepherd,' 'He shall feed his flock like a shepherd'; and when the Divine Word came to dwell among us, he chose for himself the title of the Good Shepherd, and handed it on to St. Peter, his favourite Apostle, when he committed to him the care of all the churches. He who would lead God's people must imitate the Divine forethought, the Divine patience, the Divine gentleness which tends and pursues so lovingly the straying hearts of men. Shepherd to shepherd, God delegates to Moses his pastoral office.

St. Bernadette, too, was a shepherd girl. Not that this was her business in her father's home; but when she went on a visit to friends of the family at Bartres, the year be-fore her apparitions, she was given charge of a flock of sheep, among which, characteristically, she made the tini-est lamb her favourite. So she, too, was apprenticed to

CAPTIVE FLAMES

the shepherd's trade; for she, too, was to be the leader of God's people. And the gracious Lady who appeared to her over the rose-bush, was not she the daughter of a shepherd, St. Joachim? And will not she, like Rachel before her, have fed her father's flock? Shepherdess to shepherdess, our Lady delegates to St. Bernadette her pastoral office.

Moses led his people, and they followed him, where? To the same mountain in which he had first been privileged with the intimacy of Almighty God. We were picturing, just now, a solitary figure in the desert, alone with God, no other human creature in sight. Carry your mind forward a little space of time, and you will see the same man closeted once more with the same Divine Audience; but, at the foot of the mountain, what is this? A vast array of Bedouin tents, the migration of a people. More than six hundred thousand souls worshipping God in the mountain he had chosen. With all that, the vision is still for Moses, and for Moses only. The people stand at the foot of the mountain, with limits appointed to them which they must not transgress; Moses goes up into the mountain, and is hidden by a dark cloud from mortal view. The people see the play of lightning round the summit, but the Divine Voice is not for them; it is only through Moses that the word comes to them. Yet that word is sovereign; centuries go by, and the nation of Israel increases as the sand by the seashore, but still the memory of Sinai haunts them, and their dearest traditions are all prefaced with the same rubric, 'Moses said.'

Bernadette stood before the grotto on the eleventh of February with no other human creature near her, except two little girls, her companions, on the other side of the stream. When she knelt there on the fourth of March, just three weeks later, she was being watched by a crowd of twenty thousand pilgrims. Yet still the vision was only for her; for those others there was nothing but the grotto and the rose-bush, and the mountains beyond. They could see the smile that lit up the face of the visionary, but that was all. But the memory of her smile still haunts the grotto, and all Christendom flocks there in its hundreds of thousands, to worship in the place where her feet stood. And still she haunts the place like a visible presence; when you offer your lighted candle, you half expect to hear her cry out: 'You're burning me!' as she did when she woke from her ecstasy nearly eighty years ago.

When Moses came down from the mountain, his face shone, so that the children of Israel could not bear to look upon it. They saw there, as if reflected in a frail human mirror, the glory of him who had spoken with him on the mount. And Moses covered his face with a veil, lest even that reflected radiance should be profaned by human sight.

In May, 1866, the chapel which Bernadette's ecstasies had demanded was inaugurated at Lourdes. That July she took the veil with the Sisters of Charity of Nevers, and Lourdes was not to see her again. Did we think that she would wait there to tell us all her story, to touch our rosaries and sign our autograph books? No, the face which had looked into the face of the Immaculate must be veiled thenceforward; thenceforward we should not even see her smile.

Moses was sent to deliver his people from bondage, and

from a bondage to which they had grown accustomed, so that they loved their fetters, and were constantly turning on him and asking why he could not leave them alone. That was his chief difficulty—they did not want to be set free. And even when they had been set free, and led out into the wilderness, they were always hankering after the luxuries they had enjoyed in Egypt, always murmuring against the rough fare of the desert. While Moses was up in the mountain, the people he had left behind him in the valley made a golden calf and fell to worshipping it, as they had worshipped it in Egypt. All his life he preached to an incredulous race, condemned, for their hardness of heart, to forty years' wandering in the wilderness before they achieved their promised resting-place.

Bernadette was sent to a world in bondage, and to a world which rejoiced in its bondage. Those apparitions of hers took place in the very middle of the Victorian age, when mankind, or at any rate, the richer part of mankind, was enjoying material plenty to a degree, I suppose, un-exampled before or since. And the presence of material plenty had given rise to a general spirit of materialism; a spirit which loves the good things of this life and is content with the good things of this life, does not know how to enlarge its horizons and think about eternity. She was sent to deliver us from that captivity of thought; to make us forget the idols of our prosperity, and learn afresh the meaning of suffering and the thirst for God. That is what Lourdes is for; that is what Lourdes is about—the miracles are only a by-product. You might have thought that in our day, when prosperity has waned and all of us, or nearly all of us, have to be content with less, we should have needed no longer these Divine warnings from the rock of Massabieille. We know that it is not so; we know that in this wilderness of drifting uncertainties, our modern world, we still cling to the old standard of values, still celebrate, with what conviction we may, the worship of the Golden Calf. The year of Bernadette's canonization finds us no less in need of public reparation for our common sinfulness than the year in which Bernadette took the veil.

Do not think me fanciful, then, if I suggest that we ought to see in Lourdes a sort of modern Sinai; and that we ought to treasure the words our Lady spoke in the grotto as we treasure the words God spoke to Moses on the mountain. Ten words of God to Moses, which are enshrined, now, in the general conscience of humanity; ten words of our Lady to St. Bernadette, ruling principles (surely) for the Church to whose altars the little prophetess has been raised. Let us meditate them, very briefly, as they come.

At the third apparition, St. Bernadette took with her pen and ink and a sheet of paper, to write down the commands which, she felt, the strange Lady would want to express. And the first recorded utterance of the Immaculate bears on that point; 'What I have to tell you, I do not need to set down in writing. Will you have the kindness to come here for a whole fortnight?' When Moses came down from Mount Sinai, he brought with him two tables of stone, on which the Ten Commandments had been written, we know not how, by Almighty God himself. But the Christian law, St. Paul tells us, is not written on tables of stone, but on fleshy tables of the heart. It is

not a code of directions exterior to ourselves, but a spirit
with which we are to be imbued, an attitude which we
are to assimilate. And Bernadette, accordingly, must not
expect her decalogue to be registered in pen and ink. She
must come to the grotto for a fortnight, as continuously
as she may, and the message will write itself on her heart.
And from us, too, our Lady of Lourdes asks no laborious
exercise of the intellect, no feats of memory, if we are
to learn her lesson. We are to watch Bernadette, and see
our Lady's own image in her.

That was the first word, and the second word followed
immediately, with an almost cruel abruptness: 'I do not
promise you that you will be happy in this world, but in
the next.' Moses, the servant of God, brought his people out into a land flowing with milk and honey—but he
was not allowed to enter that promised land himself. And
St. Bernadette was to open for us that miraculous spring
from which healing has flowed into thousands of homes;
the grotto in which she worshipped is hung about with a
forest of crutches, the trophies of our Lady's clients; but
St. Bernadette herself, what reward was given to her for
all her faith and endurance? Thirteen short years of life
in the cloister; years haunted with the premonition, and
crowned with the experience, of long and continued bodily suffering. We had so often been told, yet nothing really
succeeded in making us believe, that it is eternity which
matters, and time does not count. Bernadette should be a
living proof of that doctrine; our Lady's favourite confi-
dante, rewarded, not with health like us others, but with
a short life and a long cross!

At the fifth apparition, during forty minutes of ecstasy

our Lady taught St. Bernadette, word by word, a special prayer she was to use. That prayer she learned by heart, and used it every day for the rest of her life. What was it? we ask, breathlessly. The answer is that we do not know, and shall never know till, by God's grace, we are allowed to use it in heaven. The message, I say it again, was for Bernadette, and for us only through her; we are not to go to Lourdes for this or that ceremony, this or that form of prayer; it is to be the shrine not of a ritual but of a life.

And the fourth word presses on to the heart of the mystery; it was during the sixth apparition that our Lady said suddenly, 'Pray for sinners.' That is not what we think of, is it, when people ask us what are the most characteristic impressions we carried away from the Lourdes pilgrimage. We think of those wasted forms in their invalid chairs grouped round the square in the afternoon, and the heart-rending petitions that echo round them, Lord, grant that I may see, Lord, grant that I may hear, Lord, grant that I may walk. Or we think of the torchlight procession in the evening, and the singing of the Credo which concludes it; we remember Lourdes as the embodiment of a great act of faith. But when our Lady stood at the grotto, the first command she gave was not, Heal the sick; was not, Convert the unbeliever. Her command was, Pray for sinners. Man's sin, that is our real malady; man's impenitence, that is the crying problem.

The fifth word is unique, in that it was heard by the bystanders, not indeed from our Lady's lips, but from Bernadette's. As she knelt there in ecstasy, she repeated several times, sobbing, the one word, 'Penance.' They learned afterwards that she was repeating it after our Lady.

This, then, is our Lady's one public utterance; and, as I say, it is the message of Lourdes. We are to make there, in common, what reparation we can for our common faults. The true music of Lourdes is not the 'Lord, he whom thou lovest is sick' that thunders across the square; not the *Ave, Ave,* that sweeps down the terraces. It is the *Parce, Domine, parce populo tuo*—the confession of our sins, and a desperate cry for pardon.

Then, not till then, at the ninth apparition, our Lady pointed to the sacred spring, and bade her prophetess drink and wash there. This sixth word is a kind of interlude; and, remember, our Lady never said that those who drank, those who washed, would be healed of their bodily infirmities. The faithful themselves were left to find out that gracious corollary; the ceremony performed at the time by St. Bernadette was rather a pantomime of humiliation—to eat grass like the cattle, to drink and wash in a muddy spring. She dedicated herself and her mission to human scorn.

The seventh word emphasises the lesson of humiliation, and connects it with the lesson of penance. 'You will kiss the ground, for sinners.' Because all our worst sins take their origin in pride, the penance we are to offer —we moderns at least—must be prefaced by the mortification of reminding ourselves, what and whence we are. So, next Wednesday, we open our Lenten fast by having our foreheads smeared with ashes, while the priest says to us, as God said to Adam when he had sinned: 'Dust thou art, and unto dust shalt thou return.' We must learn to grovel before we can learn to weep.

With the eighth and ninth words we come at last to

practical, rubrical directions, which will serve to organize Bernadette's revelations as a cult. 'Go and tell the priests to build me a chapel'; 'I want people to come here in procession.' Man is made of body and soul; body as well as soul must take part in his self-dedication to God. Material edifices, of wood and stone, outward gestures, pilgrimage and march and song, must be the complement and the expression of his inward attitude. So, when God issued to Moses his moral law, in all the grandeur of its austerity, he directed at the same time the building of a tabernacle, and the rites which were to be performed in and at the tabernacle; he would enlist material things in the service of a spiritual ideal. So, when our Lady preached to Bernadette her gospel of penance, she externalized it and eternalized it by prescribing the outward ceremonies that should be its expression.

The tenth word is the best known of all: 'I am the Immaculate Conception.' Why (people have asked) did she say that, rather than 'I am the immaculately conceived?' It is, perhaps, rash to venture on explanations. But when God appeared to Moses, he revealed himself under the title I AM WHO AM; and theologians have read in those simple words the most profound truth about the Divine Being—that there is no distinction of Essence and Existence, of Attributes and Personality, in him; his Goodness, his Wisdom, his Power, his Justice, are nothing other than himself. That cannot be said, obviously, of any creature. But, may we not suppose that the plenitude of grace which flowed into the soul of our Blessed Lady so overshadowed and transformed her human personality as to make her little suppliant forgetful of it; make her see, there in the grotto, no longer a human figure but the embodiment of a spiritual truth? That the thought of what she was and is was obscured, in that moment of revelation, by the thought of what God wrought and works in her?

'To-day, if you will hear his voice, harden not your hearts,' was the message of Sinai. Moses struck the hard rock, and the waters gushed out; he could not wring tears, even so, from the hearts of a stubborn people. Surely, when she pointed to the miraculous spring at Lourdes, our Lady was telling a whole world to weep for its sins. So many years have passed, and do we still come away from Lourdes dry-eyed?

XX

Lisieux and Assisi

Except you shall be converted, and become as little children, you shall not enter into the kingdom of heaven (Mt 18:3).

YESTERDAY, Christendom was celebrating one of the most recent, one of the most widely loved, among the memories of God's Saints; the third of October commemorates St. Theresa of Lisieux, the Little Flower of Jesus. The prayer of the feast asks that we may follow her footsteps in humbleness and simplicity of heart. I am not absolutely certain, but I think that that is the only place in the whole of the Church's liturgy in which we pray God to make us simple. It is as if the Little Flower had discovered, for herself, a new Christian virtue. Of course, that is not really so. All the Saints have practised all the virtues, except for some of those who reached their crown through martyrdom. But it may sometimes happen that one particular virtue shines out in the life of one particular Saint more evidently than in the life of any other. The Saints, you see, are our Lord's crown; and in that crown one particular jewel catches the light, now and again, so as to shine out more than ever. All the Saints have possessed the virtue of simplicity; but it was not till God saw fit to give us a really glaring example of saintly simplicity in St. Theresa that the Church really noticed what a wonderful thing it is.

If we doubted that there was simplicity to be found among the Saints, or even that there was a high degree of simplicity to be found among the Saints, before the Little Flower came, those doubts were not able to last after October the third. October the fourth has brought with it the memory of another Saint, once more one of the most dearly loved in Christendom, who also strikes the imagination by his simplicity perhaps more than by any other gift; I mean, of course, St. Francis. In a curious way, the Poor Man of Assisi and the young nun of Lisieux stretch out hands to one another across the centuries, as if they were two children playing a children's game together— Ring a ring of roses, perhaps. I do not think it is fanciful, in spite of the difference in their centuries and their careers, to mention these two Saints in the same breath. To take just one instance, and a not very important instance—you can see the same child-like quality in each of them if you consider their fondness for make-believe. The Little Flower, you remember, when she was encouraging her novices to pray for the conversion of sinners, told them to think of those souls as a set of nine-pins, and those prayers as a ball trying to knock down first one and then another. And she was always indulging in fantasies of that kind; so was St. Francis. When he felt tempted, one extremely cold night, to regret his vows, he got up out of bed, and went out into the snow just as he was, and made a snow woman and six snow children; and he pretended that they were his wife and family. 'There,' he said to himself—for he talked to himself, as all children do—'these must all be clothed; see, poor things, they are dying of cold; here there will be all kinds of trouble.' When you read stories like that, you realize that it is not a very long way from the Little Flowers of St. Francis to the Little Flower of Jesus.

But, of course, there was all the difference in the world between the opportunities these two had of shewing their child-like qualities to the world at large. St. Theresa says in her life, addressing her superior, who was also her sister: 'An artist must have at least two brushes; the first, which is the more useful, gives the ground tints and rapidly covers the whole canvas; the other, a smaller one, is employed for the details of the picture. You, my dear Mother, represent the valuable brush our Lord holds lovingly in his hand when he wishes to do some great work in the souls of his children, and I am the little one he deigns to use afterwards to fill in the minor details.' If you will put on one side the modesty of those expressions, they give you an admirable description of the difference between St. Theresa and St. Francis. St. Theresa is the little brush; her work for God consists in etching in, very carefully, all the little daily details of a cloistered life with enormous care, like one of the pre-Raphaelite painters, drawing every leaf and every stone with minute precision. Whereas St. Francis is the impressionist; he gets his effects with broad sweeps of the brush. He will fill the world with friars, men who have a roving commission to do nothing in particular except imitate Jesus Christ; his ideas are big enough, even, to make him go off to the East and try to convert the Sultan to the Christian faith; his vision cannot be bounded by continents—that is the difference.

Not that that was a difference of temperament; rather a difference of circumstances. St. Theresa's career reminds you of those lines of Henry Vaughan:

> If a star were confined into a tomb,
>   Her captive flames must needs burn there;
> But when the hand that locked her up gives room,
>   She'll shine through all the sphere.

God locked up St. Theresa in the tomb of a Carmelite convent; he would shew a miracle of his power by making her suddenly shine through all the sphere only after she was given room, only after her bodily death. So she lived in her Carmel like a child that is shut indoors on a rainy day. She would have liked to be converting the heathen, shedding her blood as a martyr; that was not for her, so she made the best of the little world she lived in, as a child will make the best of staying indoors when it becomes clear that the rain is not going to stop. By her power of make-believe—and what it made her believe was no more than the truth—she would turn her Carmel and the little opportunities of her life at Carmel into a glorious mission for winning the souls of men. But St. Francis was different—God never locked *him* into a tomb. Think of St. Francis as you will, you always think of him as in the open air. He was a schoolboy out for a holiday, you might almost say a schoolboy playing truant from school.

All St. Francis' life was a sort of holy picnic. There is one story of his sitting down to a meal, a very simple and we should think rather an unpleasant meal, beside a spring with rocks and trees round it; and all through the meal he kept on exclaiming: 'What a treasure we have here, what a treasure!' Now, St. Francis was not one of your sophisticated modern people, who could get enthusiastic about the beauties of nature because he thought it was the proper thing to do. No, he really enjoyed the treat as a child enjoys its picnic; it was so kind of God to have arranged a setting of rocks and trees for him like that. And that is the secret, of course, of his love of creatures. Do not by the way, ever let anybody try to make you believe that St. Francis was fond of animals; he was fond of creatures. His brother was the sun, his sister the moon; when he had to have an operation on his eyes, without anæsthetics, he asked his brother fire to be gentle to him, and when the last scene of all came, he could welcome his sister death. Anybody can be fond of live animals because they remind him of human beings; grown-up people often are, and some of them are very sloppy about it. But it is the child that can manage to be fond of inanimate things, talk for hours to a stuffed bird, for example. And St. Francis was like that; he loved creatures, not because they reminded him of human beings, but because they reminded him of God.

Now, what is this gift of simplicity, which we admire so much in children, because it is natural; which we admire so much in the Saints, because it is supernatural? Do let us get rid at once of a favourite mistake; that of supposing that to be simple means to be ignorant. You see, there is only one Being who is absolutely simple; that is Almighty God, and he knows everything. No, to be simple is to see things with the eye of God, that is, to see them as they really are, without the trimmings. To be able to distinguish what is important for what is incidental and doesn't matter; to get down to the broad, primary truths, and forget what is merely conventional. I think if you asked me who was the simplest person I have ever known I should mention the name of one of the cleverest men of our generation, Mr. G. K. Chesterton, who died this summer. And it is not out of place to mention him here, because he was perhaps the best biographer St. Francis ever had, and he died when he had just come back from a visit to Lisieux. I remember he says somewhere that, if you find a man lying dead under the sofa, you explain the situation to other people by saying: There is a man lying dead under the sofa; you don't say: There is a man of considerable refinement lying dead under the sofa. On such occasions you keep to the essential facts; and that is what simplicity means, to keep to the essential facts; not just at moments, but all your life.

And for the Saint, you see, the essential facts are those of the next world, rather than those of this. God, your soul, eternity, sin, judgement, those are the essential facts; and the simplicity of the Saints is to distinguish those facts all the time, without effort, from the unessential facts that do not matter, although human vanity and snobbishness and worldliness think they do. How are we going to get that spirit ourselves? I think it is easy to see how St. Francis got it; what was the first stage, anyhow, in the getting of it. He cut himself off entirely from all worldly possessions. That is why I was telling you just now he soliloquized like that over the snow-woman, his imaginary wife. 'Here there will be all sorts of trouble,' he said to himself; he reminded himself that his vow of chastity had saved him from a whole heap of anxieties which might have distorted that simplicity of vision with which he saw God. It was the same with his poverty. When his father summoned him before the bishop, and said he would have no more to do with him and would cut him off from his inheritance, he immediately took off his clothes, because they really belonged to his father, and went about in a piece of old sacking with a cross marked on it. Now, he said, he could really understand what it was to have a Father in heaven. I have called St. Francis a truant school-boy, and that is what he was; he ran away from the world and its belongings so as to keep holiday in his heart to God.

Well, we cannot do that; our state of life and the demands which other people's lives make on our own will not allow us to do that. All right; but, remember, the less we cling to worldly enjoyments, the more we accustom ourselves to do without worldly enjoyments, the better chance we shall have of cultivating that true simplicity which is the simplicity of the Saints. The world is very old nowadays, and we are all very grown-up; you can buy the wisdom of the ages for a shilling on a bookstall; the newspapers fling problems at us, and the advertisements tell us that it is our duty to get on, to make money, and to want as much as possible. That is what we call a high standard of living, to want as much as possible. Conventions of civilization, the second servant and the fresh suit on Sundays and the latest fashion in hats and in eyebrows make life expensive for us and complicated. But with all these wonderful opportunities, is our world really a happy world? Can we look back at the age of St. Francis without feeling something of regret for our own childhood, something of that twinge which comes to us when we see, in the house where we were brought up, the familiar passage that leads to the nursery door?

The more we can resist the tyranny of these worldly embarrassments, the more we can be content to live according to our income, to be wise according to our opportunities, to be ourselves, to laugh at shams and see things as they are, the more we shall imitate St. Francis, and the better compliment we shall pay him. May his prayers, and the prayers of our Blessed Lady and St. Theresa, bring us out of this world, our schoolroom, into the glorious liberty of the sons of God.

XXI

G. K. Chesterton

Blessed are they that saw thee and were honoured with thy friendship. For we live only in our life, but after death our name shall not be such (Sir 48:11).

THE MAN whom we laid to rest the other day in the cemetery at Beaconsfield was one of the very greatest men of his time. If posterity neglects him, it will pronounce judgement not upon him, but upon itself. He will almost certainly be remembered as a great and solitary figure in literature, an artist in words and ideas with an astonishing fecundity of imaginative vision. He will almost certainly be remembered as a prophet in an age of false prophets. He warned us in spacious times that human liberties were threatened, and to-day human liberties are in debate. He warned us in times of prosperity against the perils of industrialism, and industrialism is labouring for breath. He warned us, when imperialism was a fashion, that nationalism was a force not easily destroyed; to-day nationalism is the shadow over men's hearts.

Whether he was a great author, whether he was a true prophet, does not concern him now—he lies deaf to the world's praise and secure from its catastrophes—nor does it concern us here. We are met, as Christians, to say farewell in our own fashion to a fellow-Christian who has outstripped us in the race for eternity. The most important thing about Chesterton, he would have been the first to say it, the most distinctive quality in Chesterton was a quality which he shared with some three hundred million of his fellow-men. He was a Catholic. The public discovered him in the early years of the century. It was not till twenty years later that he discovered himself. There is a legend told of his absent-mindedness that he once telegraphed home the words, 'Am in Liverpool; where ought I to be?' And it took him fourteen years after the publication of his book *Orthodoxy* to find out that he ought to be in Rome.

I hope I do not wrong such a man in preaching his panegyric, when I confine myself to considering the position which belongs to him as a religious force; what Catholicism meant to him, and what he meant to Catholicism. In the case of a meaner man we should be content to celebrate his domestic virtues, his inconspicuous acts of charity. But Chesterton moved, though with the personal simplicity of a child, in a world of apocalyptic images; he saw his religion everywhere; it mattered furiously to him. What he did is in God's hands; what he was is a matter of gracious recollection to his friends; it is the effect he made on the world that claims the world's attention and its gratitude.

I would speak first of the influence which Chesterton's earlier works had, on young men for the most part and on Protestants. And it is the only claim I have to stand here, in the place of older and closer friends, that at the time when his earlier works were published, I was myself a young man and a Protestant. I think it is true to say that the generation which grew up between the turn of the century and the Great War had a tendency all the time to react in favour of religious orthodoxy. The triumph of evolutionary materialism had seemed complete; the faith of Englishmen was laid out for burial, with the cynics, the pessimists, the positivists driving the last nails in its coffin. There was a reaction of which we should hear more if the events which began with 1914 had not decimated it and left its less characteristic specimens to represent it. I do not wish to discount the influence of other religious leaders, Anglicans like Scott Holland or Catholics like Hugh Benson. But the spear-head of that reaction was a man so plainly on the side of the angels that you did not stop to inquire whether he were an Anglican or a Catholic, G. K. Chesterton. The brilliance of his work, the wideness of his appeal set the fashion in favour of a religious attitude which the fashion of an earlier age had derided. He was conscious, himself, of the change of atmosphere when he wrote the introduction to his book, *The Man Who Was Thursday*. It is an extraordinary book, written as if the publisher had commissioned him to write something rather like the *Pilgrim's Progress* in the style of the *Pickwick Papers*. And the poem which introduces it is a song not of triumph but of release from tension in the middle of a conflict.

> 'But we were young; we lived to see God break their
>   bitter charms—
> God and the good Republic came riding back in arms;
> We have seen the city of Mansoul even as it rocked,
>   relieved—
> Blessed are they that have not seen, but, being blind,
>   believed.'

The direct effect of that reaction in stemming the tide of religious liberalism has been in great part obliterated by the War. Its indirect effect, in producing conversions to the Catholic faith, made itself felt only during the War, when the annual figure of conversions went up from eight thousand to ten and from ten to twelve, where it has remained ever since. Meanwhile the prophet, who had acted as a signpost for us, remained himself outside the Church, content to fight a lonely battle for the philosophy he could see was right but could not see was ours. What changed him then four years after the Armistice? What was the new momentum which lent impetus to his thought, so that he no longer believed, being blind, but saw? I never knew yet a convert who could give a precise answer to that question. To give a precise answer we should have to understand, as we shall never understand it here, the economy of God's grace. We can only say that if it were possible to deserve the grace of conversion, Chesterton had deserved it for years as no other man did; and, if he had to wait so long for it, there is hope in that for many a waiting soul, perhaps for some waiting soul here, which still cannot see the end of its despairs.

Meanwhile what had happened was, to Chesterton himself, admirably clear. He had the artist's eye which could suddenly see in some quite familiar object a new value; he had the poet's intuition which could suddenly detect, in the tritest of phrases, a wealth of new meanings and of possibilities. The most salient quality, I think, of his writing is the gift of illuminating the ordinary, of finding in something trivial a type of the eternal. In the first of his books which really made a name for him, *The*

Napoleon of Notting Hill, the story opens at a moment when a Government clerk, walking behind two friends in town coats, suddenly sees the buttons on their coats as two eyes, the slit underneath as a nose line; he has a vision of his two friends as two dragons walking backwards away from him. There is a law (he says in that connection) written in the darkest of the books of life, and it is this: If you look at a thing nine hundred and ninety-nine times, you are perfectly safe; if you look at it the thousandth time, you are in frightful danger of seeing it for the first time. That was all that happened when Chesterton was converted. He had looked for the thousandth time at the Catholic faith and for the first time he saw it. Nothing in the Church was new to him, and yet everything was new to him; he was like the man in his own story who had wandered round the world in order to see, with fresh eyes, his own home. That it was his home, neither friend nor foe had doubted; men did not even dare to whisper to him the old pathetic lie that converts are unhappy. Whether his work as a Catholic has been as influential as the work which he did when he was only a defender of Catholics, is a question hard to resolve. He was no longer the latest fashion; he had reached the age at which most men have had their say; his health had begun to decline, and he was overworked, partly through our fault. Nor, I think, will the world ever give a just hearing to one who has labelled himself a Catholic. But this I will say, that, if every other line he wrote should disappear from circulation, Catholic posterity would still owe him an imperishable debt of gratitude, so long as a copy of *The Everlasting Man* enriched its libraries. This I will say, that whenever I ask an inquirer whether he has read any Catholic books his answer regularly begins, 'I've read some Chesterton, of course.'

'We live only in our life and after death our name shall not be such'; few men of our time could refuse that epitaph to Gilbert Chesterton. Meanwhile 'blessed are they that saw him and were honoured by his friendship'; they found in him a living example of charity, of chivalry, of unbelievable humility which will remain with them, perhaps, as a more effective document of Catholic verity than any word even he wrote. But the familiar voice, with its high chuckle of amusement, will reach us no longer; he, whose belief in immortality was so publicly influential, can give us no whisper of reassurance, now that he knows. Only we know what we would say if he heard the suggestion that nothing remains of him beyond what was interred at Beaconsfield.

> 'The sages have a hundred maps to give;
>   They trace their crawling cosmos like a tree;
> They rattle reason out through many a sieve
>   That stores the sand and lets the gold go free.
> And all these things are less than dust to me
>   Because my name is Lazarus and I live.'

THE END